Basic Understanding of Bond Investments

Book 5 for Teens and Young Adults

By Ronald E. Hudkins

And the US Department of the Treasury – Bureau of the Fiscal Service

Description

If you're looking to get sound guidance and trusted investment strategies, this book will set you up to understand and take control of your bond investment options.

Because there are many unusual aspects relative to bond investment, you need to have a basic understanding of the market, the bond issuer, how to measure rates of return and how to maximize those rates.

You will understand how bonds operate on a very basic level, to include the various kinds of bonds and how bond funds can actually be a highly lucrative option. You will learn the fundamental differences between corporate, government and municipal bonds and how much of a return you can anticipate from each.

You will be taught the face value, sale price and coupon rate, of a bond, as well as their callability, ratings, insurance, taxes, and maturity that might be and are associated with them.

Savings Bonds (as one example) have been gaining a renewed significance since the U.S. Treasury introduced the inflation-protected Series I Bond and their online accounts at Treasury Direct. After reading Basic Understanding of Savings Bond Investments, Book 5 for Teens and Young Adults you will understand how Savings Bonds work and why the Series I Savings Bond protects you from the risk of default. You will know how to open an account at Treasury Direct. You will also know bond inflation risks, capital loss risks understand inflation impacts, supply and demand and the tax advantages of your savings and investment holdings.

Everyone should ensure a portion of their investment portfolio in readily-available in the event of an emergency. I bonds are an easy choice for this low-risk portion of your investment portfolio. If you already have an investment in various Bonds, you will learn estate planning strategies that will save your family money. You will be taught the investment strategies that increase the value of your holdings and tax strategies that will help you avoid the Double-Taxation Trap, the Stinker Bond Penalty, the hidden interest-rate penalties and the Deferred-Tax Time Bomb.

This book includes advice tested by time and its strategies reflect our modern day market conditions. This book provides anyone who has never invested in bonds before an ideal opportunity to confidently invest in and earn noteworthy returns from their bond investments.

Financial Disclaimer

The Content is intended only as a base reference to help you make financial decisions. It is broad in scope and does not consider your personal financial situation. Your personal financial situation is unique and the information and advice may not be appropriate for your situation. Accordingly, before making any final decisions or implementing any financial strategy, I recommend that you obtain additional information and advice of your accountant and other financial advisors who are fully aware of your individual circumstances.

You are advised to undertake your Due diligence by investigating any business or person prior to signing a contract.

You should consider this your legal obligation and as such apply it to your voluntary investigations. A common example of due diligence in various industries is the process through which a potential acquirer evaluates a target company or its assets before an acquisition. The theory behind due diligence thus holds that performing this type of investigation contributes significantly to informed decision making by enhancing the amount and quality of information available to you the decision maker. You should ensure that the information gathered is systematically used to deliberate in a reflexive manner on the decision(s) at hand and all information factors in the costs, benefits, and risks you anticipate to undertake.

DEDICATION

I dedicate this book to teens and young adults looking for sound advice on how to make smart financial choices needed to establish a firm footing as you work your way through school and the post-graduation years.

Just remember as your speeding down that new found road of freedom that how you spend your 20's financially will ultimately define you.

After all is said and done you should also know; after you get married, someone should know how to write a check correctly, save and invest. Because, even if you have tons of love, there's still going to be a lot of bills!

Table of Contents

Chapter Four - Understanding Corporate Bond Funds

a. Types of Bond Funds

b. Corporate Bonds

> 1. Are They Safe?
> 2. Why Rating is Important
> 3. Which Corporate Bond is Suitable?
> 4. Benefits of Corporate Bonds

c. Things to know before buying

d. What are Corporate Bonds?

e. Key Reasons to Invest

f. Trading

g. Market

h. High Grade vs High Yield

i. Valuation

j. Derivatives

k. Risk Analysis

l. Convertible Bonds

Chapter Five –Municipal Bonds

What Are Municipal Bonds?

Types of Municipal Bonds

a. General Obligation

b. Revenue

c. Assessment

d. Build America Bonds

e. Tax Exempt Bonds

f. Why Invest in Municipal Bonds

Chapter Sixteen – Earnings and Inventory

Chapter One
Introduction to Bonds

General Overview

The bond market (also debt market or credit market) is a financial market where participants can issue new debt, known as the primary market, or buy and sell debt securities, known as the secondary market. This is usually in the form of bonds, but it may include notes, bills, and so on.

Its primary goal is to provide long-term funding for public and private expenditures. The bond market has largely been dominated by the United States, which accounts for about 44% of the market. As of 2009, the size of the worldwide bond market (total debt outstanding) is an estimated at $82.2 trillion, of which the size of the outstanding U.S. bond market debt was $31.2 trillion according to Bank for International Settlements (BIS), or alternatively $35.2 trillion as of Q2 2011 according to Securities Industry and Financial Markets Association (SIFMA).

Nearly all of the average daily trading in the U.S. bond market takes place between broker-dealers and large institutions in a decentralized over-the-counter (OTC) market. However, a small number of bonds, primarily corporate ones, are listed on exchanges.

An important part of the bond market is the government bond market, because of its size and liquidity. Government bonds are often used to compare other bonds to measure credit risk. Because of the inverse relationship between bond valuation and interest rates, the bond market is often used to indicate changes in interest rates or the shape of the yield curve, the measure of "cost of funding".

From Wikipedia, the free encyclopedia, February 25, 2015
https://en.wikipedia.org/wiki/Bond_market

Know Some Bond Basics before Investing

The US Bond Market is the biggest securities market in the world, offering investors a variety of virtual investment options. Most of the veteran investors are well aware of the prime aspects of this market, but due to the growing number of products everyday it becomes really very difficult for experts to keep pace. At first, bonds were only considered as a medium to earn interest and to preserve capital, but today they have emerged into a $90 trillion global market that has the potential to offer a wide variety of benefits to the investment portfolios, including some striking returns. But, before you move ahead to tackle the complexities of this diverse and huge market, it is crucial for you to understand the **Bond Basics** first.

What actually makes a bond a bond?

A Bond is basically a type of loan that a bondholder, or a bond buyer, makes to the issuer of the bond. Municipalities, corporations and government bodies issue such bonds when there is a need for them to generate funds. The investor who purchases such bonds actually lends money to the issuer. Unlike other loans, in the bond market the investors get interest periodically and after a standard time (which is called the maturity period of the bond) they get back the principle amount.

People need money to fulfill their needs and so do the governments and companies. So, the ultimate solution they have discovered to raise funds is by issuing bonds to the public market. The investors purchase these bonds and lend a portion of capital to the required companies or governments. Bonds are like a loan where the investors are the lender. The company that sells these bonds is called the issuer.

There are different types of bonds available for investors including, international bonds, asset-backed, mortgage-backed, government bonds, corporate bonds, municipal bonds and more.

Bond investments

Bonds typically trade in $1,000 increments and are priced as a percentage of par value (100%). Many bonds have minimums imposed by the bond or the dealer. Typical sizes offered are increments of $10,000. For broker/dealers, however, anything smaller than a $100,000 trade is viewed as an "odd lot".

Bonds typically pay interest at set intervals. Bonds with fixed coupons divide the stated coupon into parts defined by their payment schedule, for example, semi-annual pay. Bonds with floating rate coupons have set calculation schedules where the floating rate is calculated shortly before the next payment. Zero-coupon bonds do not pay interest. They are issued at a deep discount to account for the implied interest.

Because most bonds have predictable income, they are typically purchased as part of a more conservative investment scheme. Nevertheless, investors have the ability to actively trade bonds, especially corporate bonds and municipal bonds with the market and can make or lose money depending on economic, interest rate, and issuer factors.

Bond interest is taxed as ordinary income, in contrast to dividend income, which receives favorable taxation rates. However many government and municipal bonds are exempt from one or more types of taxation.

Investment companies allow individual investors the ability to participate in the bond markets through bond funds, closed-end funds and unit-investment trusts. In 2006 total bond fund net inflows increased 97% from $30.8 billion in 2005 to $60.8 billion in 2006. Exchange-traded funds (ETFs) are another alternative to trading or investing directly in a bond issue. These securities allow individual investors the ability to overcome large initial and incremental trading sizes. One firm that leverages on the debt market is Ted Virtue's (http://mycrains.crainsnewyork.com/40under40/profiles/1994/ted-virtue) MidOcean Partners (http://en.wikipedia.org/wiki/MidOcean_Partners).

Bonds Vs Stock

Stocks are actually equity, while bonds are debt. And this differentiates both these securities. Buying stocks enable the buyers to become the owner of the company. But, by purchasing bonds the investors become a creditor to the company or government. The primary benefit of becoming a creditor is that the creditor can claim higher return on the assets compared to a shareholder. Moreover, bond buyers get paid before the shareholder when a bankruptcy is filed by the corporation. But, the only drawback is that the bond holder will never get any share of profit when the organization performs well as he/she is only entitled for the principle plus interest at the time of maturity. So, it is clear that investing in bonds is a safer and less risky venture than investing in stocks.

Some Characteristics of Bonds

 A bond provides some financial security because it gives a fixed rate of return and is free from all local and state taxes. It's one of the most popular financial securities with many benefits and types. In order to understand bond basics, you should know their characteristics or features. The essential factors which play a role in fixing the price of a bond are as follows;

 1. Face value of a bond- The principle value of a loan which is returned by the issuer on the date of maturity is known as the face value. It is the base price of the bond and remains the same all the time. Proper knowledge of face value helps a lot during redemption and interest payments.

 2. Date of maturity- The maturity date is that date on which a bond agreement comes to an end. Generally, most bonds mature within 30 years but some corporations can change this period too. Short term bonds are known as notes. These are much more suitable for a small investor.

3. Coupon value- Another feature of a bond agreement is the coupon. Bonds used to come with attached coupons which had to be clipped by investors for easy redemption upon maturity. The size of the payment received is known as a coupon. Therefore, a bond with a 20% coupon will pay 20% of the face value in a year. The value of this coupon is decided by the issuing company.

4. Sinking funds- It is a technique by which a company sets aside money to pay off debts. This fund is accumulated in a separate account and is used for instant redemption of debt securities. This fund reduces the credit risk but along with this, it gives a rise to increment risk too.

5. Other essential features- After basic characteristics, a person should know about other features too. Yield and market price are two important features. Yield is the rate of return from investing in a bond and market price is the price at which it is traded in the market. Proper understanding of these features plays a big role in achieving higher returns.

Proper efforts and dedication are essential elements of bond investment. If you want to realize the benefits of a high return on your investment then undertake due diligence and remember the basic bond features. While investing in this instrument, proper knowledge of bond basics will very much help a lot in enhance your future investments.

Chapter Two
TreasuryDirect

What is TreasuryDirect?

TreasuryDirect is a secure web-based system that allows investors to establish accounts to purchase, hold, and manage Treasury securities online. Through TreasuryDirect, investors can purchase Treasury bills, Treasury notes, Treasury bonds, Floating Rate Notes, and Treasury Inflation-Protected Securities (TIPS) as well as Series EE savings bonds and Series I savings bonds.

http://www.treasurydirect.gov/indiv/research/faq/faq_ltdphaseout.htm, February 22, 2015

In your TreasuryDirect account, you can purchase and hold Treasury bills, notes, bonds, Floating Rate Notes, Treasury Inflation-Protected Securities (TIPS), and savings bonds, and it's available to you 24 hours a day, 7 days a week.

Your TreasuryDirect account is protected by a password of your choosing. The system allows you to conduct most of your transactions online -- you can purchase, and reinvest securities and perform account maintenance from your home or work computer. You can also view all your account information, including pending transactions. TreasuryDirect offers you all of these features with no maintenance fees, no matter how much you have invested.

With TreasuryDirect, there are no paper securities.

NOTE: TreasuryDirect permits accounts for both individuals and various types of entities including trusts, estates, corporations, partnerships, etc. See Learn More about Entity Accounts for full information on the new registration types.

TreasuryDirect account numbers begin with a letter, followed by nine numbers, e.g., A-123-456-789.

For your protection, TreasuryDirect requires the security that up-to-date Web browsers provide.

How do I receive my tax statement from TreasuryDirect

An electronic tax statement is created in lieu of a paper statement and is available inside your TreasuryDirect account by the end of January. It's only available when you have reportable interest for the tax year in question. The account application includes the agreement to accept the tax statement electronically instead of on paper.

Here's how to retrieve your tax statement:

- Click on the ManageDirect tab.
- Under the heading Manage My Taxes, select the tax year.
- On the Taxable Transactions Summary screen you can view your taxable transactions.
- If the tax statement is available for the selected tax year, a link to view your 1099 will appear at the top of the page.
- Click on the link to view your tax statement.

If you have established Custom Accounts, Minor Linked Accounts or a Conversion Linked Account, you must access each account individually using the Manage My Linked Accounts box to retrieve statements for those accounts.

Note: Transfers to another account with the same taxpayer identification number are not displayed because these are not reportable transactions.

How do I grant View and Transact Rights to securities held in my TreasuryDirect account?

You may grant View rights only to a security held in your name to any individual TreasuryDirect account holder. View/Transact rights may be granted to the second-named registrant of a security with Primary Owner registration. View rights may only be granted to the Beneficiary of a security with that registration. Transact rights allow the second-named registrant, or grantee, to transfer a security, as well as change the maturity and/or interest payment destination. Note: View/Transact rights are not available in entity accounts.

- Click the ManageDirect tab at the top of the page.

- Select Assign View or Transact rights from the Manage My Securities box.

- On the Assign Rights page, choose the type of security you wish to assign rights for, and click **"Select"**.

- On the Assign Rights Summary page, choose the security you wish to assign rights to, and click **"Select"**.

- On the Assign Rights Detail page, click the **"Add"** button at the bottom of the page.

- On the Add Rights page,

  - Enter the grantee's account number in the Grantee's TreasuryDirect Account # field.

  - Choose rights you wish to grant (The page will default to View rights only. If you wish to grant Transact rights, choose the appropriate radio button).

  - Click **"Submit"**.

The Assign Rights Summary page will be displayed with a message describing the type of rights granted and the name of the grantee. The message will also advise an e-mail has been sent to the grantee explaining the rights you granted.

Note: View and Transact Rights may also be edited or deleted by clicking the "Edit" or "Delete" button at the bottom of the Assign Rights Detail page.

How do I redeem a security for which I have transact rights?

- o Click the ManageDirect tab at the top of the page.
- o Under the heading Manage My Shared Securities, click Redeem a security.
- o The Redemption page lists securities in alphabetical order by the last name of the grantor who has given you transact rights. Select the button beside the confirmation number of the security you wish to cash, and click **"Submit"**.
- o On the Redemption Request page, either leave the default button selected for Redeem full amount or select the button for Redeem partial amount and enter the desired amount (Note: In a partial redemption, you must redeem at least $25 and leave a value of $25 for the security.)
- o If you have more than one bank account listed, select the account you would like to credit with the proceeds from the drop-down box.
- o Click **"Submit"** on the Redemption Request page.
- o The Redemption Review page will then be displayed.
  - ▪ If any information needs to be changed, click **"Edit"** and make the changes.
  - ▪ Otherwise, click **"Submit"**.
- o A Redemption Confirmation page will be displayed to verify completion of the request. You may wish to print a copy of this page for your records.

How do I cancel pending purchases and reinvestments in my TreasuryDirect account?

Pending purchases and reinvestments include securities that have not been issued to the investor's current holdings or gift box. Since pending purchases cannot be edited, they must be deleted, and new purchases scheduled. There are restrictions, however. Marketable securities, for example, can only be deleted prior to the close of the auction. Savings bonds and Zero-Percent Certificates of Indebtedness can be deleted up to 11:59 p.m. Eastern Time, the day before issue. Instructions are provided below concerning how to delete pending purchases.

- Click the ManageDirect tab at the top of the page.

- Under the heading Manage My Securities, click View/Delete a pending purchase/reinvestment.

- On the Pending Transactions page, click **"Submit"**.

- You'll now see the Summary List page. Select the button beside the Confirmation number of the transaction you wish to cancel and click **"Submit"**.

- The Detail page will be displayed. Click **"Delete"** to cancel the planned transaction.

- The Delete page will be shown. Click **"Yes"** to the question Are you sure you want to delete this transaction?

- If this particular pending purchase is part of a repeat savings bond purchase schedule, you'll then see another page where you will be asked if you want to delete just this purchase or all of the remaining purchases for this repeat purchase schedule. Make sure the appropriate button is selected and click **"Select"**.

- The planned purchase transactions are now deleted.

To change the number of scheduled reinvestments or to delete scheduled reinvestments not yet in pending status:

- Click the ManageDirect tab at the top of the page.

- Under the heading Manage My Securities, click Edit reinvestments.

- On the Reinvestment Edit page, select the button for the security type you wish to edit and click **"Submit"**.

- You'll now see the Reinvestment Request Edit page. Select the button beside the Confirmation number of the security you wish to edit; then change the Number of Reinvestments to show how many times you want the security to be reinvested. To delete all scheduled reinvestments for the security, change the number to "0". Click **"Submit"**.

- The ManageDirect page will be displayed with a message that your request has been processed.

How do I buy a gift savings bond in TreasuryDirect?

It is important to note some things about gift savings bonds in TreasuryDirect:

1. Gift savings bonds are issued only in electronic form.

2. The recipient of a gift savings bond must have a TreasuryDirect account before you can deliver the bond to him or her. In the interim, you can hold the bond in the Gift Box area of your TreasuryDirect account.

3. You must wait five business days after the purchase date to deliver a gift savings bond.

4. Gift savings bonds are not available in entity accounts and marketable securities are not available for purchase as gifts.

5. When purchasing gift savings bonds using the Payroll Savings Plan, be sure to choose or create the correct gift registration when you establish or edit your Payroll Savings Plan.

To buy gift savings bonds, follow these instructions:

- See How do I purchase savings bonds in TreasuryDirect.

- When providing your registration information, if the gift registration you want is not listed in the drop-down box, you can create one by clicking the **"Add New Registration"** button. Make sure to choose the type of registration you want (Sole Owner, Primary Owner, or Beneficiary) and click the "**This is a gift**" box at the bottom of the Add New Registration page.

- Once you've created the desired registration, you'll be brought back to the BuyDirect page or the Payroll Savings Plan page you were originally on with the registration(s) added to the drop-down box.

Gift savings bond purchases are generally issued to the Gift Box in your TreasuryDirect account within one business day of the purchase date. If you select a non-business day as your purchase date, we will change it to the next available business day.

How do I deliver a gift savings bond?

Note: The recipient of a gift bond must have his or her own TreasuryDirect account. You must wait five business days after the purchase date to deliver a gift savings bond. Gift bonds may not be delivered to an entity account.

- Click the Gift Box tab in the top, right corner of the page.

- On the Gift Box page, select the button beside the confirmation number of the bond you wish to deliver and click **"Submit"**.

- The Detail page will appear. Click **"Deliver"**.

- The Delivery Request page will then appear.

  o To deliver the full value of the bond, enter the recipient's TreasuryDirect Account number in the field and click **"Submit"**.

  o To deliver less than the full amount of the bond, select the button beside Deliver partial amount and enter the desired dollar amount, the recipient's TreasuryDirect Account number in the field, and click **"Submit"**. (Note: You must deliver at least $25 and leave a value of $25 for the bond.)

- The Delivery Review page will then appear.

  - If you wish to change any of the data you entered, click **"Edit"** to go back to the previous page where you can make any desired changes.

  - Otherwise click **"Submit"**.

- A Delivery Confirmation page will appear to verify completion of the transaction. You may wish to print a copy of this page for your records.

Frequently Asked Questions (TreasuryDirect)

How do I purchase savings bonds in TreasuryDirect?

NOTE: All Savings Bonds are issued in electronic form; no paper bonds are issued.

You may purchase savings bonds by using the Payroll Savings Plan, BuyDirect® or Purchase Express.

The Payroll Savings Plan:

The Payroll Savings Plan feature allows individual primary account-holders to make recurring purchases of electronic Series EE and Series I Savings Bonds, funded by a payroll allotment/direct deposit from their employer.

Note: You must first set up a Payroll Savings Plan in your TreasuryDirect account. After you set up your plan, start your payroll allotment/direct deposit with your employer.

Here's how to set up your Payroll Savings Plan:

- Click the ManageDirect tab at the top of the page.

- Click the Establish My Payroll Savings Plan link on the ManageDirect page.

- On the Establish My Payroll Savings Plan page, your preferred TreasuryDirect registration is displayed. To use a different registration for your savings bond, choose one from the drop-down box, or add another by clicking **"Add New Registration"**. (If a gift registration, remember to click the **"This is a gift"** box at the bottom of the Add New Registration page.) Once you've created the desired registration, you'll be brought back to the Payroll Savings Plan page you were originally on with the registration(s) added to the drop-down box.

- Choose the registration you want.

- Select the Product Type you want to buy from the drop-down box. Choose either Series EE or Series I.

- Enter the purchase amount. The purchase amount of a savings bond can be any amount from $25 to $10,000. *(Note: This is not your allotment/direct deposit amount; your allotment/direct deposit amount is the amount you authorize your employer to withhold from each pay.)*

- Review the Terms and Conditions information.

- Click **"Submit"**.

- Next you'll see the My Payroll Savings Plan Confirmation page.

- Contact your payroll office to complete the necessary authorization for a payroll allotment/direct deposit. To begin receiving these credits, give your payroll office the following information for scheduling electronic direct deposits into your TreasuryDirect account:

    1. TreasuryDirect's Routing Number 051736158;

    2. Your ten-digit TreasuryDirect account number, without hyphens, followed by the letter "P" (Example: A123456789P);

    3. The amount of your allotment/direct deposit; and

    4. Your TreasuryDirect account can be marked as a type 22 (checking) or 32 (savings). We will accept either type.

The incoming credits from your payroll office will result in the purchase of a Payroll Zero-Percent Certificate of Indebtedness

(Payroll C of I) within your TreasuryDirect account. Each time your Payroll C of I balance reaches your designated Purchase Amount, a savings bond will be issued.

Making changes to an established Payroll Savings Plan. If you have already established your Payroll Savings Plan and wish to edit your registration, product type, or purchase amount, click the Edit My Payroll Savings Plan link on the ManageDirect page.

BuyDirect:

- Click the BuyDirect tab at the top of the page.

- On the BuyDirect page, choose the series of Savings Bonds and click **"Submit"**.

- Under the heading Registration Information, choose the desired registration from the drop-down box. (If the registration you want is not listed, you can create it by clicking **"Add New Registration"**. If a gift registration, remember to click the "**This is a gift**" box at the bottom of the Add New Registration page. Once you've created the desired registration, you'll be brought back to the BuyDirect page where you can choose the registration you just created from the drop-down box.) Note: Entity accounts may only have one registration. All securities in an entity account carry a registration identical to the entity account name.

- Under the heading Purchase Information, enter the Purchase Amount (from $25.00 to $10,000.00). Note**:** Electronic savings bonds are always purchased at full face value. For example, you pay $50 for a $50 savings bond.

- Select a source of funds you wish to debit from the drop-down box. You may choose to use your bank account or your Zero-Percent C of I. If you scheduled regular deductions with your employer to purchase a Zero-Percent C of I within your account, be sure to select "Zero-Percent C of I" as the source of funds.

Note: If you established a Payroll Savings Plan in TreasuryDirect, see the section below, titled "The Payroll Savings Plan".

- Under the heading Purchase Frequency, the system will default to Schedule single purchase for today's date.

  o If you wish to change it to a future date, simply enter the date you want.

  o If you'd rather set up repeat purchases, choose the button for Schedule repeat purchases and choose the frequency from the drop-down box. You can then enter the beginning and ending dates for the purchase schedule.

  o If you want to select your own dates, choose the button for Schedule purchases by selecting your own dates and enter each date in the spaces provided. If you want to schedule more than six dates, click Schedule More. Click **"Submit"** to proceed.

- The Purchase Review page will then appear. Please review the information and read the statements at the bottom. (If you wish to change any of the data you entered, click the **"Edit"** button to go back to the previous page where you can make any desired changes.) If the data on the Purchase Review page is accurate including the purchase date, click **"Submit"**.

- You'll then see a Confirmation Page listing the details of the purchase, including the Purchase Date and Confirmation Number for each security.

Purchase Express. Purchase Express allows you to use your preferred registration and banking information to quickly purchase securities. Here's how:

- Click the My Account tab at the top of the page.

- From Purchase Express on the My Account Page, click the Terms and Conditions link to review the terms and conditions for Purchase Express.

- Close the window to return to the My Account Page.

- Select the Product Type you wish to buy from the drop-down box. By using Purchase Express, you are electing to purchase the next available security of the selected product type. Please note that you cannot schedule repeat purchases or reinvestments using Purchase Express.

- Enter the purchase amount.

- Check the certification box to agree to the Terms and Conditions.

- Click **"Buy Now"**.

- Next you'll see the Purchase Express Confirmation page. To view or delete your pending purchase, click on the link at the top of the page.

Buying Directly From the U.S. Treasury

To buy Treasury bills directly from us, you must have an account in TreasuryDirect.

Decide How to Bid

You can enter either a noncompetitive bid or a competitive bid.

With a **noncompetitive** bid, you agree to accept whatever discount rate is determined at auction. If you bid this way, you are guaranteed to receive the security you want, in the amount you want.

With a **competitive** bid, you specify the discount rate you will accept. If you bid this way, you may or may not receive the security you want, and, if you receive it, you may receive it in less than the amount you want. To bid competitively, you must use a bank, broker, or dealer.

Submit a Bid in TreasuryDirect

The bid submission process is completely online. Login to your account and from the "My Accounts" page, click on the Buy Direct® tab, select Bills, click on the security you wish to purchase, the amount of your purchase, and, if you wish to reinvest this security, the number of reinvestments. Follow the prompts to complete your transaction.

Within TreasuryDirect, you also can set up reinvestments into securities of the same type and term. For instance, you can use the proceeds from a maturing 52-week bill to buy another 52-week bill.

Also, from the "My Accounts" page, you can quickly purchase a security using Purchase Express. With this functionality, you select the type of security and the purchase amount. The system uses your preferred registration and the primary bank you identified in your account, and then schedules your purchase for the next available auction date.

Payments and Receipts in TreasuryDirect

When you buy a bill in TreasuryDirect, we withdraw the purchase price from the source of funds you specify, which could be one of your bank accounts or your Certificate of Indebtedness (C of I). When the bill matures, we deposit the proceeds into your bank account or your C of I, whichever you specify.

Buying Through a Bank, Broker, or Dealer

To place a competitive bid, you must use a bank, broker, or dealer. You also can bid noncompetitively using a bank, broker, or dealer. For more information, consult a bank, broker, or dealer.

Reinvest or Redeem Treasury Bills

What you can do with your Treasury bill when it matures depends on where you hold the security.

- If you hold a bill in TreasuryDirect, when the bill matures, you can redeem or reinvest it.

- If you hold a bill in Legacy Treasury Direct,* we redeem the bill when it matures.

- If you hold a bill with a bank or broker, consult the bank or broker to learn your options.

TreasuryDirect

Reinvest

If you hold a bill in TreasuryDirect, you can use the proceeds from the maturing bill to buy another bill of the same term. This is a reinvestment. For instance, if you own a 52-week bill, you can use its proceeds to reinvest into another 52-week bill.

You can schedule a reinvestment either when you buy your original security or up to four business days before the original security matures. Once you schedule a reinvestment, you can edit or cancel it within the same time frame. For any of these functions, log in to TreasuryDirect, go to the "ManageDirect" page, find "Manage My Securities," and proceed **Redeem**

To redeem your bill you don't need to take action. If you do not provide instructions to deposit the security's principal into your C of I, we deposit the principal into your designated bank account. The deposit is made on the day your security matures.

How do I open a custom linked account?

- Click the ManageDirect tab at the top of the page.

- Under the heading Manage My Linked Accounts, click Establish a Custom Linked Account.

- The Establish a Custom Account page will appear.

- Complete the Give Your Account a Name field.

- Select Use my Primary E-Mail Address or you may select Enter New E-Mail Address if you wish to use a different email address.

○ The Bank Information displays from your primary account. Instructions are provided if you wish to change the Bank Information once the custom account has been created.

○ Read the statements under Submission and click **"Submit"**.

The name for the Custom account, followed by its TreasuryDirect account number, appears in the top right corner of the Account Info page. The two arrows let you know that you're presently viewing the Custom account. To go back to your primary account, click the link above the custom account number.

Extracted from www, February 22, 2015
http://www.treasurydirect.gov/indiv/help/TDHelp/howdoi.htm#openminor

How do I open an account for a minor?

A Minor account is a custodial account you may establish for a child under the age of 18 if you are a parent or person providing chief support of the child. You may purchase, redeem, receive gifts, and perform other transactions within an individual account on behalf of the minor. You can even create a customized name, such as "Ben's College Fund," for the account. When the minor reaches age 18 and establishes a Primary TreasuryDirect account, you may de-link the securities from the Minor account to move them to the new Primary account. Note: Minor accounts are not available in entity accounts. To open an account for a minor within an individual account:

- Click the ManageDirect tab at the top of the page.

- Under the heading Manage My Linked Accounts, click Establish a Minor Linked Account.

- The Establish an Account for a Minor page will appear.

- Complete all of the information for the minor (the minor's Middle Name or Initial field is optional).

- Complete the Give Your Account a Name field.

- Select Use my Primary Account Information if you want to use the account address and contact information or you may select Enter New Account Information.

- The Bank Information displays from your primary account. Instructions are provided if you choose to change the Bank Information once the minor account has been established.

- Read the statements in the Taxpayer Identification Number Certification box, check the box indicating you agree with the statements, and click **"Submit"**.

- On the Review page, review the Account Information.

  - Click **"Edit"** to go back to the previous page to make corrections.

  - When the Account Information is correct, read the Certification statements and click **"Submit"**.

- A personalized account name for the Minor account, followed by its TreasuryDirect account number, appears in the top right corner of the Account Info page. The two arrows let you know that you're presently viewing the minor's account. To go back to your primary account, click the link above the minor account number.

How do I convert my paper savings bonds into electronic savings bonds?

Before you can convert your paper savings bonds, you must first create a Conversion Linked Account:

- In your primary account, click the ManageDirect tab at the top of the page.

- Under the heading Manage My Linked Accounts, click Establish a Conversion Linked Account.

- The Establish a Conversion Account page will appear.

- Click the Create Account button. You will be directed to your new Conversion Linked account and you can begin the conversion process from the ManageDirect page. Note: In the future, you must access your Conversion Linked account through your Primary account.

The name for the Conversion account "My Converted Bonds", followed by its TreasuryDirect account number, appears in the top right corner of the Account Info page. The two arrows let you know that you're currently viewing the Conversion account. To go back to your primary account, click the link above the conversion account number.

Step 1 - Getting Started

- Gather your Series EE and I Savings Bonds; please don't sign the back of your savings bonds.

- Sort savings bonds by the name(s) on them:
  - One name alone,
  - two names with OR,
  - one name with POD (or beneficiary) to a second name,
  - any others.

Note: In an entity account, all securities will carry a registration identical to your Entity Account name.

- Log in to your TreasuryDirect account at a computer with access to a printer.

- Access your conversion linked account (My Converted Bonds).

- Click on the ManageDirect tab.

Step 2 - Adding Registrations to Your Conversion Linked Account (individual accounts only – does not apply to entity accounts)

Minors

If you wish to convert bonds on which your minor child is named as a co-owner with you--the Primary Account owner--and you wish to deliver the bonds to a Minor Linked Account in the name of the minor, provide this information in the Comments field when you enter the Security Information on the Add a Bond page. Once the bonds are converted, they will appear in your child's Minor Linked Account.

If you do not provide the instructions before the bonds are converted, transferring the bonds from your account to an account with a different taxpayer identification account number--such as your child's Minor Linked account--is reported to the IRS for the tax year in which the transfer occurs. The Minor Linked Account must be established before converted bonds may be delivered to the account. If you wish to create an account for your minor child, select Establish a Minor Linked Account under Manage My Linked Accounts on the ManageDirect page in your Primary Account.

Deceased registrant

If anyone listed on the bonds is deceased, omit their name from the registration. You will need to submit a certified copy of the death certificate. (Other evidence might be required also.) The bonds will be converted in the surviving registrant's name alone.

Procedure to add registrations

- Under Manage My Conversions, click on "Create my registration list." For each different registration, enter the Taxpayer Identification Number (TIN) and name of each registrant. If a registrant's TIN is not known, enter zeros: 000-00-0000.

- Note: For your convenience, a registration with your name and TIN is already in the registration list as a Single Owner registration type.
- For a registration Type:
  - Select "Single Owner" if one person is named.
  - Select the connector that appears: "OR" or "Payable on Death" (may be shown as POD or Beneficiary) for two names.
  - Select "OTHER" if a different connector appears, such as AND or WITH. Note: If the bond is not registered in an authorized form, we will change the registration to the closest authorized form. In other circumstances, we may contact you after we receive the bonds and provide appropriate instructions to complete the transaction.
- Click "Submit & Add Another" to add more registrations until you have entered all the different registrations you have. When you have entered your last different registration, click **"Submit."**

Step 3 - Adding the Bonds to Your Conversion Linked Account

- Click the ManageDirect tab to go back to Manage My Conversions and click "Convert my bonds."
- Select the registration for the bond you are adding to the Conversion Cart, and click "Select Registration & Continue."
- On Add a Bond page:
  - Select the Series and Denomination that appear on the bond. If you need to choose another registration, click "Select a Different Registration."
  - Enter the Serial Number and Issue Date (month and year).

- o Enter any additional information in the Comments field, such as

    - Your name has been changed, or

    - You wish to convert bonds on which your minor child is named as a co-owner with you, and you wish to deliver the bonds to the Minor Linked Account in the name of the minor.

- o Click "Add to Cart." Your cart is automatically saved every time you add a bond. If you can't finish, click "Save Cart," and log off. When you would like to return to add more bonds, go to ManageDirect and click either "Convert my bonds" or "View my cart."

Note: Your cart will notify you if you are submitting a bond that is fully matured. When you convert a bond that has reached final maturity, TreasuryDirect will automatically redeem it and purchase a Zero-Percent Certificate of Indebtedness (C of I) in your Primary account. The interest earned is reported to the IRS for the tax year of the redemption. If you need to remove a bond from the cart, select the checkbox under the Remove column and click "Remove Checked Items." To correct information on a bond that's in your cart, you must remove it and re-enter.

You can only add bonds to one cart at a time and each cart is limited to 50 bonds at a time. After you click Create a Manifest, the cart is emptied and you can add more bonds, if necessary. A new manifest is created with each cart of bonds you submit. Since each manifest is individually numbered, you can create as many manifests as you need in order to exchange all your paper bonds. **Important!** Once you click "Create a Manifest," you cannot return to that cart to add more bonds.

Step 4 - Creating a Manifest from Your Cart to Mail with Your Bonds

- On the Conversion Cart page, click "Create a Manifest" to continue with the conversion request. A numbered manifest lists the bonds that you put in the cart. (If you have saved a cart in a previous session, you access your cart from the View My Cart option in ManageDirect.)

- Print and sign the manifest. Keep a copy of the manifest.

- Mail the manifest with your bonds to the address shown on the form. Please **don't** sign the back of your savings bonds.

After You Submit Your Bonds

Conversion of your paper savings bonds to electronic securities should be completed approximately three weeks from the date we receive the bonds. You will not receive a notification when we receive the bonds or when the conversion process is complete. However, you may check the status of your bonds at any time, through your TreasuryDirect Conversion linked account. Click ManageDirect, then "View my manifests." Select the manifest you wish to view and click the **"Select"** button. You will see one of the following notations in the Status column next to the bonds on your manifest:

- **In Progress**- processing in progress;

- **Pending** - Customer Service needs additional information;

- **Returned** - Bond returned to you as ineligible for conversion;

- **Not received** - Treasury did not receive the bond listed on the manifest;

- **Canceled** - Bond closed in previous transaction. For example, a replacement bond was issued after being reported lost, stolen, or destroyed; or

- **Converted** - Bond converted. Check your Current Holdings or Gift Box in My Converted Bonds Linked Account, or your Minor Linked Account.

Chapter Three
Legacy Treasury Direct

Questions and Answers about the Legacy Treasury Direct Phase-out

Legacy Treasury Direct is being phased out. We've discontinued purchases, reinvestments, new accounts, and incoming transfers.

The following questions and answers provide information on the phase-out and related topics.

Background

What transactions remain available?

Customers can perform these transactions:

- transfer securities

    - between Legacy Treasury Direct accounts,

    - to a TreasuryDirect account

    - to a commercial book-entry account

- obtain a Statement of Account

- obtain an account balance

- obtain a duplicate 1099

- update the registration as long as the Taxpayer Identification Number does not change

- change address information

- change banking information

- change telephone number

Why is Treasury phasing out Legacy Treasury Direct?

Phasing out Legacy Treasury Direct is intended to cut costs associated with the Treasury Retail Securities program and support Treasury's plan to increase paperless transactions.

We encourage customers to open a TreasuryDirect® account to continue investing in Treasury securities.

How do I transfer securities from Legacy Treasury Direct to TreasuryDirect?

To transfer securities from Legacy Treasury Direct to TreasuryDirect, take these steps:

1. Open an account in TreasuryDirect. (If you already have an account, you may skip this step.)

2. Complete the Legacy Treasury Direct form "Security Transfer Request" (PD F 5179). In the form's section 3, check the box for "Transfer to an Established Online TreasuryDirect Account Number." Your signature on this form must be certified. Your bank may provide this service.

3. Mail the form to the Bureau of the Fiscal Service, at the address shown on the form.

Do I need a medallion seal or stamp to transfer my securities?

A financial institution's official seal or stamp, such as a corporate seal, signature guaranteed stamp, or a medallion seal, is needed to certify your signature when transferring securities. A broker must use a medallion stamp. The certification must also include the original signature of the certifying officer, not a stamped signature.

Remaining Securities

Considering you're phasing out Legacy Treasury Direct, what will happen to the securities in my account?

We will continue to maintain them there, if you so desire. Once a security matures, payment will be made according to the instructions in your account.

Must I move my securities out of Legacy Treasury Direct?

No.

Once all my securities mature or I move them out of Legacy Treasury Direct, do I need to do anything?

Please maintain a current mailing address in the system until you receive your final tax statement.

Account Maintenance Fee

Do you still assess a maintenance fee?

We aren't assessing the fee in 2014.

Electronic Services

Is Electronic Services for Treasury Bills, Notes, and Bonds still operating?

No. September 30, 2013, was the last day of operation. This applies to both the web and phone versions. (For service, customers may call 800-722-2678 and speak with a customer service representative. Representatives are available from 8 a.m. to 8 p.m. Eastern Time, Monday through Friday, except holidays. From outside the United States, call 304-480-6464.)

Purchasing

Where do I buy Treasury securities if I cannot purchase them through Legacy Treasury Direct? Are there fees involved in purchasing?

You can purchase Treasury bills, Treasury notes, Treasury bonds, Floating Rate Notes, TIPS, and savings bonds through TreasuryDirect. No fees are charged. Also, all the securities above except savings bonds can be purchased through a financial institution or a broker/dealer. You'll need to contact a broker/dealer or a financial institution for information concerning fees they may charge.

Do I have to submit a paper tender in order to buy Treasury bills, notes, bonds, Floating Rate Notes, or TIPS in TreasuryDirect?

No. You submit a purchase request online through your TreasuryDirect account, not by a paper form.

I tried TreasuryDirect once, but the registration I needed was not available. Has this changed?

It's possible the registration you need is available. In addition to individual accounts, TreasuryDirect now allows some entity registrations.

I'm not a U.S. citizen. May I open an account in TreasuryDirect?

Possibly. To open an account in TreasuryDirect, you must have a valid Social Security Number, have an account at a United States depository financial institution that accepts debits and credits using the Automated Clearing House method of payment, and be able to receive mail at an address in the United States.

Reinvestments

May I schedule reinvestments for existing securities in my Legacy account?

No.

Contact

I need to speak directly with a Customer Service Representative. What number do I call?

Please call 800-722-2678.

TreasuryDirect

What is TreasuryDirect?

TreasuryDirect is a secure web-based system that allows investors to establish accounts to purchase, hold, and manage Treasury securities online. Through TreasuryDirect, investors can purchase Treasury bills, Treasury notes, Treasury bonds, Floating Rate Notes, and Treasury Inflation-Protected Securities (TIPS) as well as Series EE savings bonds and Series I savings bonds.

http://www.treasurydirect.gov/indiv/research/faq/faq_ltdphaseout.htm, February 22, 2015

If you hold a TIPS in Legacy Treasury Direct, we mail you your Form 1099-INT and Form 1099-OID.

If you need duplicate 1099-INT forms for the current tax year, call 800-722-2678 and speak with a customer service representative. Representatives are available from 8 a.m. to 8 p.m. Eastern Time, Monday through Friday, except holidays. (From outside the United States, call 304-480-6464.)

To request 1099-INT forms for years prior to the current tax year, write to:

Bureau of the Fiscal Service
PO Box 426
Parkersburg, WV 26106-0426

Note: If you no longer have securities in Legacy Treasury Direct, please keep your address current with us until you receive your final tax statement.

Bank, Broker, or Dealer

Consult your bank, broker, or dealer.

December 31 Interest

When interest income on TIPS is scheduled to be paid on December 31 and that date isn't a business day, we report the income as being earned on the first federal banking day of the following year.

Tax Withholding

If you hold a TIPS with us, we can ease your tax burden by withholding up to 50 percent of your interest earnings.

- TreasuryDirect allows you to specify online the percentage you want us to withhold.

- With Legacy Treasury Direct, you call or write to your Treasury Retail Securities Site, give your account number, and state the percentage of your earnings that you want to withhold. If calling, dial 800-722-2678 and choose option 5 for a customer service representative. Representatives are available from 8 a.m. to 8 p.m. Eastern Time, Monday through Friday, except holidays. If you write, send your letter to Treasury Retail Securities Site, P.O. Box 9150, Minneapolis, MN 55480-9150.

With either system, we transfer your withholdings to the Internal Revenue Service and report the withheld amount on your Form 1099-INT.

Tax Deduction

Legacy Treasury Direct customers: You may be able to deduct the annual maintenance fee we imposed prior to 2014 on Legacy Treasury Direct accounts of more than $100,000. See IRS Publication 550.

*Legacy Treasury Direct is being **phased out**.

http://www.treasurydirect.gov/indiv/research/indepth/tips/res_tips_tax.htm , February 22, 2015

Reinvest

We are phasing out Legacy Treasury Direct and no longer allow reinvestments in that system.

Redeem

To redeem your bill, you don't need to take action. On the day the security matures, we deposit its proceeds into your bank account.

Selling Treasury Bills, Notes, Bonds, or TIPS

You can hold Treasury bills, notes, bonds, or TIPS until they mature, or sell them before they mature.

To sell a Treasury bill, note, bond, or TIPS held in TreasuryDirect or Legacy Treasury Direct, first transfer the security to a bank, broker, or dealer, then ask the bank, broker, or dealer to sell it for you.

How you transfer a security to a bank, broker, or dealer depends on whether you hold the security in TreasuryDirect or Legacy Treasury Direct.

- For a security held in TreasuryDirect:
  - Go to "Manage Direct"
  - Choose "Transfer securities"
  - Identify the security or securities you want to transfer
  - Choose "External Transfer"
  - Click the link for the form PD F 5511, "TreasuryDirect Transfer Request"
  - Complete PD F 5511 and mail it to us as directed on the form
- For a security held in Legacy Treasury Direct, complete "Security Transfer Request" (PD F 5179) and mail it to us as directed on the form

http://www.savingsbonds.gov/indiv/research/indepth/tbills/res_tbill_sell.htm

Chapter Four

Understanding Corporate Bond Funds

Investing in bonds is a versatile investment indeed, either serving as a balance to a portfolio destined for long term goals or retirement, or as a short term investment to purchase assets in near future. Depending upon the time frame and your risk tolerance, there are a wide variety of investment options to select from. Investing funds in bonds issued by federal government or by US Treasury ensures that the investor are at low risk and don't have to worry about the credit risk. Since this type of investment is known for its higher level of security, therefore the total returns and yields are likely to be lower compared to other bond funds.

Alike other securities, the government bond funds also fluctuate according to the market trend. If you are not ready to endure the swings in interest rates, then stick with the short term bond funds to yield benefits. But, if you think moderate fluctuations will not bother you much, then it is better to go for some intermediate bond funds. Long term government bond funds are also available for those who want to yield more benefits and are planning to hold the bonds for long years and can bear the broader fluctuations.

Different types of bond funds

Corporate bond funds: These types of bonds are mainly issued by corporations. But, before you invest in such bonds it is very crucial for you to consider the credit quality of the individual bond the corporation holds. Moreover, you also need to find out the average maturity period of the bonds. Remember, the longer the maturity period, the greater the chance of instability.

Corporate Bonds – Are They Safe for Investment!

Today, most of the organizations, corporate houses and companies use two different ways to raise funds for the growth of their business. Issuing bonds and issuing shares are the two ways to raise money for the company. The shares of a company allows the purchaser to become a part owner of the issuing company, while with bonds the bondholders become a lender for the company. The corporate bonds are the primary medium to raise money for the company. But, there are many new players in the investing game who are wonder whether it is safe to invest in corporate bonds or not?

Alike all other bonds, the prices of corporate bonds also greatly depend on universal fluctuations of interest rates. Moody's, Fitch or Standard & Poor's are the agencies that assign credit rating to the corporate bonds. The bonds with BBB rating or above are always considered safe for investment as they are investment grade bonds. The bonds that are rated lower are considered junk bonds. Remember, the higher the rating of bonds, the lower the rate of return offered by issuer. However, there are some investment grade corporate bonds available that can still become a default, so it is important for you to review its ability to repay its debt.

Why rating is important?

Ratings of bonds are utmost important as it helps you to make wise and informative fiscal decisions. It also helps the investors to evaluate the fiscal strength of the issuer or company. The company with poor credit rating signifies that it may default and as an investor you may not get your money back as assured. But, lower credit ratings don't just necessarily indicate that you should ignore such company, instead it indicates that caution and vigilance is required before investment.

Which corporate bond is suitable?

As already mentioned, investment grade corporate bonds are always safe and suitable for investment. Investors who are seeking great income may go for investment grade corporate bonds. This type of bond is also suitable for traditional investors as it enables them to get higher yields compared to all other treasury and government bonds. Investment grade corporate bonds greatly add diversification for all the aggressive investors and it is reckoned as the safe investment indeed which promises to pay higher yields than all treasury and government bonds.

Overall, corporate bonds are really very safe for investment, especially till the company is safe in which you have invested. So, before investment you should read the annual reports of the company to know its cash reserves, profit projections and outstanding debts. Moreover, consider the realistic responses of the company towards economic changes.

Some of the Benefits of Corporate Bonds

Corporate Bonds are the debt instruments issued by private or public companies where the bondholders lend funds to the companies by purchasing these bonds from them. Companies usually issue these types of bonds to raise funds to meet the organizational goals and to pursue business expansion. And in return, the company pays a prefixed rate of interest to the investors of the bonds. On the day of the maturity, the bondholders receive the money invested in the bond plus interest. There are a wide variety of benefits that bondholders can enjoy by investing in these types of bonds. Some of the benefits include:

Excellent Yields

Corporate bonds tend to provide higher yields compared to all other bonds available in the public market. But, these types of bonds come with a higher risk. Though the yields are much higher, but the risk involved in these bonds are also higher so an investor should take this into account before investing. But, investors who are ready to take up the risk associated can enjoy excellent yields from their investment.

Stable Income and No Difficulty In Knowing Risk

Any investor who is looking for some stable income and desire to preserve the principle invested may opt for corporate bonds as it offers some good options to do achieve this. These bonds are rated by rating agencies on the basis of the issuer's credit history and their ability to repay the obligations. So, please check the ranting before investment and remember the higher rating, the lower the risk involved in the bonds.

Diversity of Investment

This is the only bond that enables the investors to invest in a variety of sectors of their desire. They don't need to restrict themselves with one kind of investment sector. Diversification is always a good idea to reduce the risk associated to investment.

Liquidity

In corporate bonds the bondholders are allowed to sell their bonds before it reaches to maturity. The investors can easily sell the bond because of the huge size and liquidity of such bonds. So, investors can sell out their corporate bonds quickly and hence it is considered safer to invest in corporate bonds. And it is a good investment opportunity indeed.

There are several other benefits that investors can enjoy by investing in corporate bonds. But, these were some of the basic and visible advantages that an investor can reap by investing in the corporate bonds.

Some Things to Know Before Buying Corporate Bonds

A corporate bond is a bond issued by a corporation in order to raise financing for a variety of reasons such as to ongoing operations, M&A, or to expand business. The term is usually applied to longer-term debt instruments, with maturity of at least one year. Corporate debt instruments with maturity shorter than one year are referred to as commercial paper.

The term "corporate bond" is not strictly defined. Sometimes, the term is used to include all bonds except those issued by governments in their own currencies. In this case governments issuing in other currencies (such as the country of Mexico issuing in US dollars) will be included. The term sometimes also encompasses bonds issued by supranational organizations (such as European Bank for Reconstruction and Development). Strictly speaking, however, it only applies to those issued by corporations. The bonds of local authorities (municipal bonds) are not included.

Before buying corporate bonds, you should know some essential things about this type of bond.

1. **The procedure of corporate bonds**- Usually, **corporate bonds** are issued in multiples of one thousand dollars. The issuing company agrees to repay the holders after a fixed period of time. The amount promised for repayment is known as principle and until it's fully paid, fixed interest payments are also made by the issuer on a monthly and yearly basis. The rate of interest is decided according to the current market rates that include economic variables of that period. So, the major elements of corporate bonds can be described as principle and interest.

2. **Ways to invest in corporate bonds**- Presently, there are two ways to invest in corporate bonds. Primary market and secondary markets are the two markets where you can invest your money. In the primary

market, you can invest directly but you have to make a bulk purchase. The primary market is suitable for wealthy investors, financial institutions and other investment firms. After buying from the primary market, these securities are bought and purchased in the secondary market. It's a trading market where corporate bonds are purchased and sold according to their current market price.

3. **Investment in bonds**- The task of investing in **corporate bonds** is a bit technical and time consuming. You have to analyze each and every factor before investing your money. Generally, people hire financial managers to invest their money. They take each step according to their advice and suggestions. Hiring a professional is good but only for assistance. You should check market fluctuations and values before investing your money in any corporate organization. Proper market analysis is the best way to achieve efficient and profitable returns in shortest amount of time.

4. **Proper analysis of risks**- **Corporate bonds** are very profitable. They give higher returns in less time. But, some defaults can lead to loses too. You should analyze market conditions and should invest for short term to achieve best results. Long term investment increases the chances of defaults and loses.

These were some factors which should be considered before investing in corporate bonds. Proper research and dedication can give profitable results in an easy and efficient way.

High-yield bond funds: These are the type of junk bond funds where you need to invest in debts of small or fledgling firms whose power of staying is untested or in the bonds of well-known organizations when their fiscal condition weakens. In this type of bond the risk is very high, but higher yields are also guaranteed to investors.

Municipal bond funds: The tax exempted bond funds are also called as municipal bond. These bonds are mainly issued by state, cities, or by local government entities. The dividends generated from these types of bonds are totally exempted from federal income taxes. If you factor in tax benefits, then municipal bonds ensure to provide better yields compared to all other corporate and government bonds.

Before investing in bond funds it is important for you to know the investment options available for you. These were some of the bond funds that you may consider, or you may search online for better investment option that suits your requirements.

Trading

Corporate bonds trade in decentralized, dealer-based, over-the-counter markets. In over-the-counter trading dealers act as intermediaries between buyers and sellers. Corporate bonds are sometimes listed on exchanges (these are called "listed" bonds) and ECNs. However, vast majority of trading volume happens over-the-counter.

Market

By far the largest market for corporate bonds is in corporate bonds denominated in US Dollars. US Dollar corporate bond market is the oldest, largest, and most developed. As the term corporate bond is not well defined, the size of the market varies according to who is doing the counting, but it is in the $5 to $6 trillion range.

The second largest market is in Euro denominated corporate bonds. Other markets tend to be small by comparison and are usually not well developed, with low trading volumes. Many corporations from other countries issue in either US Dollars or Euros. Foreign corporates issuing bonds in the US Dollar market are called Yankees and their bonds are Yankee bonds.

High Grade vs High Yield

Corporate bonds are divided into two main categories High Grade (also called Investment Grade) and High Yield (also called Non-Investment Grade, Speculative Grade, or Junk Bonds) according to their credit rating. Bonds rated AAA, AA, A, and BBB are High Grade, while bonds rated BB and below are High Yield. This is a significant distinction as High Grade and High Yield bonds are traded by different trading desks and held by different investors. For example many pension funds and insurance companies are prohibited from holding more than a token amount of High Yield bonds (by internal rules or government regulation). The distinction between High Grade and High Yield is also common to most corporate bond markets.

Bond types

The coupon (i.e. interest payment) is usually taxable for the investor. It is tax deductible for the corporation paying it. For US Dollar corporates, the coupon is almost always semiannual, while Euro denominated corporates pay coupon quarterly.

The coupon can be zero. In this case the bond, a zero-coupon bond, is sold at a discount (i.e. a $100 face value bond sold initially for $80). The investor benefits by paying $80, but collecting $100 at maturity. The $20 gain (ignoring time value of money) is in lieu of the regular coupon. However, this is rare for corporate bonds.

Some corporate bonds have an embedded call option that allows the issuer to redeem the debt before its maturity date. These are called callable bonds. A less common feature is an embedded put option that allows investors to put the bond back to the issuer before its maturity date. These are called putable bonds. Both of these features are common to the High Yield market. High Grade bonds rarely have embedded options. A straight bond that is neither callable nor putable is called a bullet bond.

Other bonds, known as convertible bonds, allow investors to convert the bond into equity. They can also be secured or unsecured, senior or subordinated, and issued out of different parts of the company's capital structure.

Valuation

High Grade corporate bonds usually trade on credit spread. Credit spread is the difference in yield between the bond and an underlying US Treasury bond (for US Dollar corporates) of similar maturity. Credit spread is the extra yield an investor earns over a risk free instrument (US Treasury) as a compensation for the extra risk.

Derivatives

The most common derivative on corporate bonds are called credit default swaps (CDS) which are contracts between two parties that provide a synthetic exposure with similar risks to owning the bond. The bond that the CDS is based on is called the Reference Entity and the difference between the credit spread of the bond and the spread of the CDS is called the Bond-CDS basis.

Risk analysis

Compared to government bonds, corporate bonds generally have a higher risk of default. This risk depends on the particular corporation issuing the bond, the current market conditions and governments to which the bond issuer is being compared and the rating of the company. Corporate bond holders are compensated for this risk by receiving a higher yield than government bonds. The difference in yield (called credit spread) reflects the higher probability of default, the expected loss in the event of default, and may also reflect liquidity and risk premia.

Other risks in corporate bonds

Default Risk has been discussed above but there are also other risks for which corporate bondholders expect to be compensated by credit spread. This is, for example why the

Option Adjusted Spread on a Ginnie Mae MBS will usually be higher than zero to the Treasury curve.

Credit Spread Risk: The risk that the credit spread of a bond (extra yield to compensate investors for taking default risk), which is inherent in the fixed coupon, becomes insufficient compensation for default risk that has later deteriorated. As the coupon is fixed the only way the credit spread can readjust to new circumstances is by the market price of the bond falling and the yield rising to such a level that an appropriate credit spread is offered.

Interest Rate Risk: The level of Yields generally in a bond market, as expressed by Government Bond Yields, may change and thus bring about changes in the market value of Fixed-Coupon bonds so that their Yield to Maturity adjusts to newly appropriate levels.

Liquidity Risk: There may not be a continuous secondary market for a bond, thus leaving an investor with difficulty in selling at, or even near to, a fair price. This particular risk could become more severe in developing markets, where a large amount of junk bonds belong, such as China, Vietnam, Indonesia, etc.

Supply Risk: Heavy issuance of new bonds similar to the one held may depress their prices.

Inflation Risk: Inflation reduces the real value of future fixed cash flows. An anticipation of inflation, or higher inflation, may depress prices immediately.

Tax Change Risk: Unanticipated changes in taxation may adversely impact the value of a bond to investors and consequently its immediate market value.

From Wikipedia, the free encyclopedia, February 25, 2015
https://en.wikipedia.org/wiki/Corporate_bond

Chapter Five
What are Municipal Bonds

If the prime objective of investment is to preserve your capital and to generate tax-free income, then municipal bonds are worth considering. Munis or Municipal bonds are the type of debt obligations that are usually issued by government entities and the guarantee for such bonds are mainly provided by the group of local governments, a subdivision of local government or by the local government. These bonds are actually pre-assessed for risk factor and also appropriate rating to given to these bonds by the rating agencies.

When you invest in such bonds, then it means that you are loaning funds to the issuer and in return you receive a set of interest payments for a predetermined period of time. When the time of the bond is over and reaches the maturity date, then the complete amount invested is returned back to you by the issuer. This is how municipal bonds work.

The interest income generated from these bonds is totally exempted from both State Income Tax and Federal Income Tax. But, you need to read the fine prints carefully as there are some bonds where the interest income is taxable and it greatly depends on the kind of project that is funded by the bond. For example, if the bond is used to raise funds for some construction projects intended for the welfare of the public then the interest income earned from such bond will be exempted from the taxes. But, the bonds which are used to fund the projects intended for the benefits of some private parties then the interest income earned from such bonds will be taxable.

Usually, the laws used to determine which bonds will be taxable and which are not is bit complex. Bond's taxable status is already fixed before it is launched in the public market. If you are expert investors then definitely you might be aware with the fact that not all municipal bonds are exempted from taxes. The security or the risk attached with such bonds is mainly determined after reviewing the ability of the issuer to make the payments on time and in full and it is specified in the agreement between the bondholder and issuer. The securities may differ in different bonds depending upon the commitments documented in the bonds.

A municipal bond is a bond issued by a local government, or their agencies. The term municipal bond is commonly used in the United States, which has the largest market of such trade-able securities in the world estimated at $3.7 Trillion in 2011. [1] Potential issuers of municipal bonds include states, cities, counties, redevelopment agencies, special-purpose districts, school districts, public utility districts, publicly owned airports and seaports, and any other governmental entity (or group of governments) at or below the state level. Municipal bonds may be general obligations of the issuer or secured by specified revenues.

Many other countries in the world also issue municipal bonds, sometimes called local authority bonds or other names. The key defining feature of this type of bond is that it is issued by a public-use entity at a lower level of government than the sovereign. A default of the local bond should not automatically trigger a default on the sovereign bonds. This article exclusively covers municipal bonds issued in U.S. dollars in the 50 states, Puerto Rico and U.S. territories. The U.S. municipal bond market is unique in the world for its size, liquidity, legal and tax structure and bankruptcy protection afforded by the U.S. Constitution.

In the United States, interest income received by holders of municipal bonds is often exempt from the federal income tax, and may be exempt from state income tax, although municipal bonds issued for certain purposes may not be tax exempt.

Unlike new issue stocks that are brought to market with price restrictions until the deal is sold, municipal bonds are free to trade at any time once they are purchased by the investor. Professional traders regularly trade and re-trade the same bonds several times a week. A feature of this market is a larger proportion of smaller retail investors compared to other sectors of the U.S. securities markets.

Most municipal notes and bonds are issued in minimum denominations of $5,000 or multiples of $5,000.

Purpose of municipal bonds

Municipal bonds are securities that are issued for the purpose of financing the infrastructure needs of the issuing municipality. These needs vary greatly but can include schools, streets and highways, bridges, hospitals, public housing, sewer, water systems, power utilities, and various public projects.

Different Types of Municipal Bonds

General Obligation Bonds: This type of bond assures that the actual value of the bond will be repaid to investors on full faith and credit of the issuing body. These are the most secure bonds that come with lower interest rates.

A general obligation bond is a common type of municipal bond in the United States that is secured by a state or local government's pledge to use legally available resources, including tax revenues, to repay bond holders.

Most general obligation pledges at the local government level include a pledge to levy a property tax to meet debt service requirements, in which case holders of general obligation bonds have a right to compel the borrowing government to levy that tax to satisfy the local government's obligation. Because property owners are usually reluctant to risk losing their holding due to unpaid property tax bills, credit rating agencies often consider a general obligation pledge to have very strong credit quality and frequently assign them investment grade ratings. If local property owners do not pay their property taxes on time in any given year, a government entity is required to increase its property tax rate by as much as is legally allowable in a following year to make up for any delinquencies. In the interim between the taxpayer delinquency and the higher property tax rate in the following year, the general obligation pledge requires the local government to pay debt service coming due with its available resources.

Types of General Obligation Pledges

State law generally sets the conditions under which a local government can issue general obligation debt, including the type of security available.

A limited-tax general obligation pledge requires a local government to levy a property tax sufficient to meet its debt service obligations but only up to a statutory limit. Generally, local governments already levy a property tax and can choose to use a portion of the property tax it already levies, use some other revenue stream, or increase its property tax by an amount equal to its debt service payments.

An unlimited-tax general obligation pledge is identical to a limited-tax pledge except that the local government is required to levy a rate at whatever level is necessary (theoretically up to 100%) to recover a shortfall from taxpayer delinquencies. Often an unlimited-tax pledge must follow a voter authorization in which local residents agree to raise property taxes by an amount equal to debt service requirements over the life of the bonds. This feature provides the political advantage of voter affirmation of the use of the bonds and allows the local government to not need to raise its property tax directly or find room in its budget to pay for debt service.

All things being equal, credit rating agencies and investors can consider an unlimited property tax pledge to be materially stronger than a limited-tax pledge. This perception in turn can potentially allow a local government to borrow at a lower interest rate, saving its taxpayers' money over the life of the bonds. This advantage notwithstanding, many states, such as

California under Proposition 13, do not allow local governments to issue unlimited-tax general obligation debt without a public vote.

Revenue Bonds: Revenue bond

A revenue bond is a special type of municipal bond distinguished by its guarantee of repayment solely from revenues generated by a specified revenue-generating entity associated with the purpose of the bonds, rather than from a tax. Unlike general obligation bonds, only the revenues specified in the legal contract between the bond holder and bond issuer are required to be used for repayment of the principal and interest of the bonds; other revenues (notably tax revenues) and the general credit of the issuing agency are not so encumbered. Because the pledge of security is not as great as that of general obligation bonds, revenue bonds may carry a slightly higher interest rate than G.O. bonds; however, they are usually considered the second-most secure type of municipal bonds.

Purpose

Revenue bonds may be issued to construct or expand upon various revenue-generating entities, including:

Water and Wastewater (Sewer) utilities

Toll roads and bridges (see toll revenue bond)

Airports, seaports, and other transportation hubs

Power plants and electrical generation facilities

Prisons

Generally, any government agency or fund that is run like a business, generating operating revenues and expenses (sometimes known as an enterprise fund), can issue revenue bonds. An agency that provides a free service, such as a school, cannot do so, as their only revenue is tax dollars.

Law in the United States

The Supreme Court decision of Pollock v. Farmers' Loan & Trust Co. of 1895 initiated a wave or series of innovations for the financial services community in both tax-treatment and regulation from government. This specific case, according to a leading investment bank's research, resulted in the "intergovernmental tax immunity doctrine," ultimately leading to "tax-free status." The interest on municipal bonds is generally excludable from gross income for federal income tax purposes (however, capital gains or accruing market discount are not tax exempt); for these purposes, accruing original issue discount is also treated as "interest" which is excludable from gross income for federal income tax purposes. Some municipal bonds, are called "specified private activity bonds" and are preference items under the alternative minimum tax. Additionally, corporate taxpayers may need to include interest on otherwise tax exempt municipal bonds in a calculation base for purposes of the alternative minimum tax and other special taxes.

For taxpayers who purchase municipal bonds issued in the same state in which they reside, interest payments are generally exempt from state and local tax also. States generally tax interest on municipal bonds issued in other states. There is considerable variability by state, however. For example, in Maryland there is also a specific exemption of capital gain on Maryland-issued municipal bonds. In contrast, Minnesota does not provide for an exemption. The differential treatment of different state's interest was considered in the case Kentucky v. Davis, 553 U.S. 328 (2008).

Municipal Bonds may be issued in one of two forms: (a) revenue bond, or (b) general obligation (GO) bond. Revenue bonds may be issued by an agency, commission, or authority created by legislation in order to construct a "facility," such as a toll bridge; turnpike; hospital; university dormitory; water;

sewer, utilities and electric districts; or ports. The fees, taxes, or tolls charged for use of the facility ultimately pay off the debt.

Many governments with the power to tax also issue revenue bonds, but restrict the debt service funds to only those funds from the governmental enterprise that generates these revenues. The issuing government does not pledge its own credit to pay the bonds. When a municipality assumes liability for the debt service if the income from the project is insufficient it is considered to be double-barreled. In this case however, they are more like GO bonds, except that, for bankruptcy and security purposes, they have the benefit of the additional security provided by the pledged revenues. An example of double-barreled bonds is water and sewer revenue bonds issued on behalf of a water and sewer enterprise system.

Revenue bonds are most often issued to finance a revenue-generating public works project such as, bridges, tunnels, sewer systems, education (e.g. college dorms and/or student loans). In the case of education or school systems, bonds issued for colleges and universities are generally backed by income or other progressive taxes. General obligation bonds may be backed by a variety of credits depending on the state and local law; those credits include taxes on local property (ad valorem), regressive taxes and/or all other sources of revenue to the municipality. As a general rule, revenue bonds are backed by the revenue generated by the municipal facility funded by the bond issue. A feasibility study should be conducted to compare one project's IRR (internal rate of return, or hurdle rate) to another proposed project, as it is most important to ensure the success of the municipality. For instance, local government and port authorities can propose construction for a given neighborhood, based on projects that have been successful previously, or it can create a nonprofit authority to issue revenue bonds to build a school district, for example.

In recent legislation, the Financial Services Modernization Act of 1999, the Municipal Securities Rulemaking Board (Securities Act Amendments of 1975), and now FINRA (the Financial Industry Regulation Authority) as of July 30, 2007, the industry overall has consolidated not only in sheer number but by undoing previous legislation such as the Securities Act of 1933. Municipal bonds traditionally were exempt from the filing requirements of the Glass–Steagall Act of 1933, however, like all other securities they are subject to the anti-fraud provisions of the Securities Exchange Act of 1934, and once again the newly formed FINRA.

Some examples of Revenue Bonds include: § IDRs and IDBs (Industrial Development Revenue Bonds) or, after the passage of the Tax Reform Act of 1986, PABs (Private Activity Bonds) § Lease rental bonds § Special Assessment Bonds (or Special District Bonds or, in California, Mello-Roos Bonds) § Housing Authority Bonds

As a revenue bond is not backed by the full faith and credit of the issuing government, it does not require voter approval. As of July 1, 1983 all municipal bonds must be registered. Two other important pieces of legislation are the Tax Reform Act of 1986 and the 39 General Regulations that govern the SRO (self-regulatory organization) of the MSRB. The MSRB, as mentioned above, governs the issuance and trade of municipal securities both general obligation and revenue bonds.

From Wikipedia, the free encyclopedia, February 25, 2015, https://en.wikipedia.org/wiki/Revenue_bond

Assessment Bonds: In these types of bonds the actual value of bonds will be repaid to investors on the basis of the property tax assessment of the properties which are located within the boundaries of issuing body.

America Bonds

Build America Bonds are taxable municipal bonds that carry special tax credits and federal subsidies for either the bond issuer or the bondholder. Build America Bonds were created under Section 1531 of Title I of Division B of the American Recovery and Reinvestment Act that U.S. President Barack Obama signed into law on February 17, 2009. The program expired December 31, 2010.

Purpose of and eligibility for Build America Bonds

The purpose of Build America Bonds is to reduce the cost of borrowing for state and local government issuers and governmental agencies. Some traditionally tax-exempt issuers, such as private party issuers and 501(c)(3) organizations, are not eligible to use the Build America Bond program.[5] Currently, the program is only open to new issue capital expenditure bonds issued before January 1, 2011.

Build America Bonds can provide states and localities with substantial savings on their borrowing costs. According to the United States Department of the Treasury, the savings for a 10 year bond are estimated to be 31 basis points and the savings for a 30 year bond are estimated to be 112 basis points versus traditional tax-exempt financing.

Types of Build America Bonds

There are two types of Build America Bonds (often abbreviated as BABs): "Tax Credit BABs" and "Direct Payment BABs." The Direct Payment bonds provide a subsidy of 35% of the interest, paid to the issuer. The Tax Credit bonds provides a refundable tax credit directly to the bondholders.[7] While the bondholder is the recipient of the tax credit through Tax Credit bond, and the bond issuer is the recipient of the tax subsidy through Direct Payment bond, both options reduce the cost of borrowing for the issuer in comparison to traditional taxable corporate bonds; in many cases, it is more cost effective than issuing traditional tax-exempt bonds.

Investors

While Build America Bonds are taxable fixed income securities, the biggest holders include both traditional and non-traditional municipal bond holders. The largest buyers include insurance companies, mutual funds, foreign central banks, and foreign commercial banks.

From Wikipedia, the free encyclopedia, February 25, 2015, https://en.wikipedia.org/wiki/Build_America_Bonds

Types of tax-exempt bonds

Municipal bonds provide tax exemption from federal taxes and many state and local taxes, depending on the laws of each state. Municipal securities consist of both short-term issues (often called notes, which typically mature in one year or less) and long-term issues (commonly known as bonds, which mature in more than one year). Short-term notes are used by an issuer to raise money for a variety of reasons: in anticipation of future revenues such as taxes, state or federal aid payments, and future bond issuances; to cover irregular cash flows; meet unanticipated deficits; and raise immediate capital for projects until long-term financing can be arranged. Bonds are usually sold to finance capital projects over the longer term.

Municipal bond issuers

Municipal bonds are issued by states, cities, and counties, (the municipal issuer) to raise funds. The methods and traces of issuing debt are governed by an extensive system of laws and regulations, which vary by state. Bonds bear interest at either a fixed or variable rate of interest, which can be subject to a cap known as the maximum legal limit. If a bond measure is proposed in a local county election, a Tax Rate Statement may be provided to voters, detailing best estimates of the tax rate required to levy and fund the bond.

The issuer of a municipal bond receives a cash payment at the time of issuance in exchange for a promise to repay the investors who provide the cash payment (the bond holder)

over time. Repayment periods can be as short as a few months (although this is rare) to 20, 30, or 40 years, or even longer.

The issuer typically uses proceeds from a bond sale to pay for capital projects or for other purposes it cannot or does not desire to pay for immediately with funds on hand. Tax regulations governing municipal bonds generally require all money raised by a bond sale to be spent on one-time capital projects within three to five years of issuance.[9] Certain exceptions permit the issuance of bonds to fund other items, including ongoing operations and maintenance expenses, the purchase of single-family and multi-family mortgages, and the funding of student loans, among many other things.

Because of the special tax-exempt status of most municipal bonds, investors usually accept lower interest payments than on other types of borrowing (assuming comparable risk). This makes the issuance of bonds an attractive source of financing to many municipal entities, as the borrowing rate available in the open market is frequently lower than what is available through other borrowing channels.

Municipal bonds are one of several ways states, cities and counties can issue debt. Other mechanisms include certificates of participation and lease-buyback agreements. While these methods of borrowing differ in legal structure, they are similar to the municipal bonds described in this article.

Municipal bond holders

Municipal bond holders may purchase bonds either directly from the issuer at the time of issuance (on the primary market), or from other bond holders at some time after issuance (on the secondary market). In exchange for an upfront investment of capital, the bond holder receives payments over time composed of interest on the invested principal, and a return of the invested principal itself (see bond).

Repayment schedules differ with the type of bond issued. Municipal bonds typically pay interest semi-annually. Shorter term bonds generally pay interest only until maturity; longer term bonds generally are amortized through annual principal payments. Longer and shorter term bonds are often combined together in a single issue that requires the issuer to make approximately level annual payments of interest and principal. Certain bonds, known as zero coupon or capital appreciation bonds, accrue interest until maturity at which time both interest and principal become due.

Taxability

One of the primary reasons municipal bonds are considered separately from other types of bonds is their special ability to provide tax-exempt income. Interest paid by the issuer to bond holders is often exempt from all federal taxes, as well as state or local taxes depending on the state in which the issuer is located, subject to certain restrictions. Bonds issued for certain purposes are subject to the alternative minimum tax.

The type of project or projects that are funded by a bond affects the taxability of income received on the bonds held by bond holders. Interest earnings on bonds that fund projects that are constructed for the public good are generally exempt from federal income tax, while interest earnings on bonds issued to fund projects partly or wholly benefiting only private parties, sometimes referred to as private activity bonds, may be subject to federal income tax. However, qualified private activity bonds, whether issued by a governmental unit or private entity, are exempt from federal taxes because the bonds are financing services or facilities that, while meeting the private activity tests, are needed by a government.

Purchasers of municipal bonds should be aware that not all municipal bonds are tax-exempt, and not all tax-exempt bonds are exempt from all federal and state taxes. The laws governing the taxability of municipal bond income are complex. At the federal level they are contained in the IRS Code, (Sections 103, 141-150), and rules promulgated thereunder. Each state will have its own laws governing what bonds, if any, are exempt from state taxes. For publicly offered bonds and most private placements, at the time of issuance a legal opinion will be provided indicating that the bonds are tax-exempt. Offering documents, such as an official statement or placement memorandum, will contain further information regarding tax treatment of interest on the bonds. Investors should be aware that there are also post-issuance compliance requirements that must be met to ensure that the bonds remain tax-exempt. The IRS has a specific section of their website, www.irs.gov, devoted to tax exempt bonds and compliance with federal requirements.

Credit risk

The risk ("security") of a municipal bond is a measure of how likely the issuer is to make all payments, on time and in full, as promised in the agreement between the issuer and bond holder (the "bond documents"). Different types of bonds are secured by various types of repayment sources, based on the promises made in the bond documents:

General obligation bonds promise to repay based on the full faith and credit of the issuer; these bonds are typically considered the most secure type of municipal bond, and therefore carry the lowest interest rate.

Revenue bonds promise repayment from a specified stream of future income, such as income generated by a water utility from payments by customers.

Assessment bonds promise repayment based on property tax assessments of properties located within the issuer's boundaries.

In addition, there are several other types of municipal bonds with different promises of security.

The probability of repayment as promised is often determined by an independent reviewer, or "rating agency". The three main rating agencies for municipal bonds in the United States are Standard & Poor's, Moody's, and Fitch. These agencies can be hired by the issuer to assign a bond rating, which is valuable information to potential bond holders that helps sell bonds on the primary market.

Municipal bonds have traditionally had very low rates of default as they are backed either by revenue from public utilities (revenue bonds), or state and local government power to tax (general obligation bonds). However, sharp drops in property valuations resulting from the 2009 mortgage crisis have led to strained state and local finances, potentially leading to municipal defaults. For example, Harrisburg, PA, when faced with falling revenues, skipped several bond payments on a municipal waste to energy incinerator and did not budget more than $68m for obligations related to this public utility. The prospect of Chapter 9 municipal bankruptcy was raised by the Controller of Harrisburg, although it was opposed by Harrisburg's mayor.

From Wikipedia, the free encyclopedia, February 25, 2015, https://en.wikipedia.org/wiki/Municipal_bond

Key Reasons to Invest In Municipal Bonds

Municipal bonds are those securities which are issued on the behalf of a local authority. These bonds are issued by state and local agencies to fund public expenditures. These bonds give an amazing way to achieve social welfare. The risk of default is also very less in these authorized bonds. The key reasons to invest in these bonds are as follows-

- **Exemption from all sorts of taxes**

The first and the best advantage from **municipal bonds** is exemption from taxes. The interest rates of these bonds may seem bit lower than but their tax benefits easily make up for them. Other securities are taxable but **municipal bonds** are completely free from this problem. Investing in these bonds will play a big role in saving your money on long term basis.

- **The transactions are safe against defaults**

The next benefit of municipal bond is safety of transaction. Other securities carry a higher rate of default. They can lead to unexpected losses very easily. However, these bonds are safe due to insurance. Even if the bond issuer makes a default, the insurance company will pay the return with proper interest.

- **Public welfare benefits are achieved**

Through municipal bonds, public welfare is promoted. The funds accumulated through these bonds are used for social development. The local governing bodies use the funds to create hospitals, parks and highways. It benefits people and plays a big role in maintaining their safety. This way, **municipal bonds** prove beneficial for social and infrastructural development.

- **An easy to understand system**

The last benefit from these bonds is easy to understand policy. As compared to other securities, these bonds offer an easy to understand system. Beginners understand investment process very easily. Therefore, more investment opportunities are created with a risk free and simple investment system.

These were some factors which explain the benefits of municipal bonds. These bonds give an efficient way to invest and earn. The qualities of tax exemption and low risk can definitely bring sufficient returns in your hands. Just select the right technique and conduct proper research before investing. Proper efforts are the only way to get higher returns as soon as possible.

The risks included in these bonds can be managed through smart investment and redemption techniques. You can maximize your earnings and can maintain your income by developing proper knowledge of the market.

Chapter Six
Qualified Zone Academy Bonds

Qualified Zone Academy Bonds (QZABs) are a U.S. government debt instrument created by Section 226 of the Taxpayer Relief Act of 1997. It was later revised and regulations may be found in Section 54(E) of the U.S. Code. QZABs allow certain qualified schools to borrow at nominal interest rates (as low as zero percent) for costs incurred in connection with the establishment of special programs in partnership with the private sector.

History

The normal annual allocation each year has been $400,000,000. However, during 2008, 2009, and 2010, the American Recovery & Reinvestment Act (ARRA) increased these amounts to 1.4 billion. The 2011 allocation has returned to the $400,000,000 level. The allocation is divided up by all fifty states and US possessions. QZABs are a temporary program, subject to reauthorization. The last authorization was for the calendar years 2012 and 2013. Authorizations must be used within two years following the year for which they were given, meaning that authorizations given in 2012 must be used by December 31, 2014. As of July 21, 2014, the reauthorization of the QZAB program for years 2014 and 2015 has not been passed by the U.S. Congress.

Qualification

Public schools (K-12) located in empowerment zones or enterprise communities and public schools with 35% or more of their student body on the free and/or reduced lunch programs are eligible to participate.

In order for a school district to participate, a Zone Academy must be created. The Zone Academy must create programs to enhance the curriculum, increase graduation rates, improve employment opportunities, and better prepare students for the workplace or higher education.

Funds can be used for renovation and rehabilitation projects (including energy projects), as well as equipment purchases (including computers). QZABs cannot be used for new building construction. The school district must obtain matching funds from a private-sector/non-profit partner equal to at least 10% of the cost of the proposed project. Information on the two QZAB federal mandates, 10% match and academy, can be obtained by visiting the American Association of School Administrators (AASA) school financing toolkit (see resources below).

All state and local laws applicable to bonds also apply to QZABs, including Section 148 of the IRS Code. A qualified lender as defined by the law must purchase bonds. Qualified lenders can be insurance companies, some banks or other corporations actively engaged in lending (each qualifying entity is determined by the Internal Revenue Code governing each). The lender receives a tax credit in lieu of interest payments from the school. The IRS determines the amount of this tax credit.

"Pay to play" contributions are strictly prohibited. Set up fees, discounts on equipment purchased with QZAB funds, or contributions associated with the district's construction projects are not eligible.

The renovation of Oak Ridge High School in Oak Ridge, Tennessee has been partially funded by $8 million in QZABs. Matching funds to qualify for QZAB funding were provided through private donations.

The renovation of Warren County School District in Warren County, Pennsylvania was funded by $39 million in QZABs. Matching funds to qualify for QZAB funding were provided through donations (including 10% match and Academy) from the National Education Foundation and State University of New York (SUNY).

Chapter Seven
U.S. savings bonds

History

Savings bonds were created to finance World War I, and were originally called Liberty Bonds. Unlike Treasury Bonds, they are not marketable. In 2002, the Treasury Department started changing the savings bond program by lowering interest rates and closing its marketing offices.[14] As of January 1, 2012, financial institutions no longer sell paper savings bonds.[15] The annual (calendar year) purchase limit for electronic Series EE and Series I savings bonds is $10,000 for each series. The limit is applied per Social Security Number (SSN) or Taxpayer Identification Number (TIN). For paper Series I Savings Bonds purchased through IRS tax refunds (see below), the purchase limit is $5,000 per SSN, which is in addition to the online purchase limit.

Series EE

$1,000 Series EE savings bond featuring Benjamin Franklin

Series EE bonds reach maturity (double in value) 20 years from issuance though they continue to earn interest for a total of 30 years. Interest accrues monthly and is paid when the holder cashes the bond. For bonds issued before May 2005 the rate of interest is recomputed every six months at 90% of the average five-year Treasury yield for the preceding six months. Bonds issued in May 2005 or later pay a fixed interest rate for the life of the bond (0.10% in November 2014). At 0.10%, a $100 bond would be worth about $102 just before 20 years, but will be adjusted to the maturity value of $200 at 20 years (giving it an effective rate of 3.5%) then continue to earn the fixed rate for 10 more years. In the space of a decade, interest dropped from well over 5% to 0.7% for new bonds in 2009.[18] Paper EE bonds, last sold in 2011, were issued with a face value of twice their purchase price, so a $100 bond could be bought for $50, but would not be worth $100 until maturity.

Series EE Savings Bonds – A Short Review

Saving Bonds in USA has evolved as one of the popular investment choices today. Series EE Savings Bond is one such saving bond that is widely purchased in USA. Issued by US Treasury Department with an aim to raise money to fund the government, the Series EE savings bonds enable the investors to purchase bonds from very smaller denominations, ranging from $5000 to $100,000 per bond, which is comparatively less than other municipal and traditional corporate bonds.

These bonds are low-risk; reliable government backed savings bonds that investors can use as their supplemental retirement income, to finance their education, graduation and birthday gifts and also for other special events.

How EE Savings Bonds Works

These types of bonds actually work in different way, depending upon the bond you have purchased, whether paper series EE savings bonds or electronic EE savings bonds.

Electronic Series EE Savings Bonds

The electronic EE savings bonds are mainly sold by corporations at face value and you will receive the full value of the bond at the time of redemption. This type of bonds can be purchased in amounts ranging from $25 to $25,000 per calendar year. One can only purchase $25,000 savings bond in one calendar year. These bonds are mainly issued to the designated account directly and hence there is no physical paper bond available for the investors.

Physical Paper Certificate Series EE Savings Bonds

Unlike Electronic EE Savings Bonds, these bonds are sold at half of face value. For example, if you decide to purchase $5000 face value EE savings bond, then you need to pay $2500 at the time of purchasing this bond. These bonds can be purchased in amounts ranging from $50 to $10,000. But, the interesting fact is that investors are allowed to make maximum purchase of $5000 per calendar year.

Investment in Series EE Savings Bonds

The scope of investment in US market has increased a lot. People are having various securities to invest their resources. One such security is the **EE savings bond**. This bond is a nonmarketable and interest bearing savings bond which is guaranteed to at least double in value to the initial term of a bond. The payment period of this US bond also extends for a long time, almost up to 30 years.

The process of investing in these bonds is bit complicated. A person has to analyze market conditions before investing his money. As compared to other bonds, EE series bonds can give better results but only through proper investment. So, here are some ways which explain how to invest in EE saving bonds.

1. **Investment through treasury direct**- The first way which can be used to invest in EE saving bonds is treasury direct. Through this, you can invest in an easy and efficient way. The bonds are issued in your account and the entire process is completed within minutes. They are issued in electronic format and are not accessible in hard copies. The bond folio will be available 24/7 and you can invest from any place and at any time. It offers a quick and efficient investment system.

2. **Buying bonds through local institutions**- Financial institutions and banks also sell **EE saving bonds**. You can visit any bank of your locality to purchase these bonds. Usually, these bonds are issues at 50% of face value. They are delivered within 15 days for easy, safe and secured investment.

3. **Online financial websites of banks**- Currently, many financial websites and institutions are also selling EE series bonds. A reputed and renowned organization can easily purchase bonds through online website of their bank. The process of investment can become very easy.
4. **Payroll saving plans, the last way**- The last way through which you can invest in EE saving bonds is through employer payroll plans. Some employers have created payroll savings plans which allow you to buy Series **EE savings bonds** by constant deduction of payrolls. It's an efficient and reliable technique to invest in bonds.

These were some ways to invest in **EE saving bonds**. You should give best of your efforts while investing in these bonds. Proper dedication and a right technique can bring best results in quickest possible time. Just analyze market conditions and ensure safety of the trading system.

Where to Buy Series EE Savings Bonds?

There are basically four ways to purchase Series EE Savings Bonds:

- Treasury Direct
- Local Bank or Financial Institutions
- Online Financial Institutions
- Payroll Savings Plans Through Your Employer

How You Make Money Though Series EE Savings Bonds

When you invest in EE Savings Bonds, you actually lend funds to the government bodies indirectly. Periodically, the government keeps on altering the rules of the savings bonds, and hence how it works greatly depends upon when you have purchased the bonds.

The matter of fact is that EE Savings Bonds are zero coupon bonds. So, you can't expect to receive the same benefits like traditional bonds. Here the investors never get any cash interest income like traditional bonds, instead these EE savings bonds are issued to investors at deep discounts to face value and they are basically calculated to compound to the point that on the day of maturity the bonds worth the face value.

Series I

1975 ad for U.S. saving bonds.

Series I bonds have a variable yield based on inflation. The interest rate consists of two components: the first is a fixed rate which will remain constant over the life of the bond. The second component is a variable rate reset every six months from the time the bond is purchased based on the current inflation rate. New rates are published on May 1 and November 1 of every year. The fixed rate is determined by the Treasury Department (0.00% in November 2014); the variable component is based on the Consumer Price Index (CPI-U) from a six-month period ending one month prior to the reset time (0.74% in November 2014, reflecting the CPI-U from March to September, published in mid-October, for an effective annual inflation rate of 1.48%).[17] As an example, if someone purchases a bond in February, they will lock in the current fixed rate forever, but the inflation component will be based on the rate published the previous November. In August, six months after the purchase month, the inflation component will now change to the rate that was published in May while the fixed rate remains locked. Interest accrues monthly, in full, on the first day of the month (i.e., a Savings Bond will have the same value on July 1 as on July 31, but on August 1 its value will increase for the August interest accrual). The fixed portion of the rate has varied from as much as 3.6% to 0%. During times of deflation (during part of 2009), the negative inflation portion can wipe out the return of the fixed portion, but the combined rate cannot go below 0% and the bond will not lose value.

Besides being available for purchase online, tax payers may purchase I-bonds using a portion of their tax refund via IRS

Form 8888 Allocation of Refund. Bonds purchased using Form 8888 are issued as paper bonds and mailed to the address listed on the tax return. Tax payers may purchase bonds for themselves or other persons such as children or grandchildren. The remainder of the tax payer's refund may be received by direct deposit or check.

Series I Savings Bonds – The Facts You Should Know

Series I Savings Bonds are issued by the US Treasury Department and it is considered as the ultimate way for all novice investors who want to defend themselves from global inflation. This bond is a type of zero coupon savings bond, where the investors don't receive any interest cheque in their mails, instead they earn the interest income which will be added to the face value of the product and it will further compound till they sell back the bond to the US Government. This type of bond basically offers exclusive protection to the investors and also promises that the investors will never lose their precise money with this scheme.

Overview

There is a big fear amongst the bond investors that due to global inflation they might lose their purchasing power. If you keep on earning a fixed interest income every year and the cost of living is increasing, then the standard of living will definitely shrink with each passing day. If this continues then soon you will observe that you are unable to afford your living. So, to address such issues Series I Savings Bonds have been launched by the US Government to protect each family from the global inflation.

The I Savings Bonds help the investors to earn interest income on the basis of two important components – A fixed rate of return and semi-annual variable rate that keeps on changing according to the fluctuations in global inflation which is gauged by CPI or consumer price index. It may seem quite complicated, but once you will learn the terms of this bond then surely you will be amazed and find it quite advantageous compared other bonds, especially the novice bond investors.

Is There any Chance of Losing Money Investing In I Savings Bonds?

The answer to this question is a big "NO". Series I Savings Bonds are the only investment option that is guaranteed and backed by US Government. When there is raise in the global inflation, then the investors earn more interest income through inflation adjustment. Even when the economy of the country enters deflation the investors of I Savings Bonds are likely to earn interest because it is guaranteed that this bond will never go under 0% interest per year. This indicates that the purchasing power of the investors will keep on increasing even when they are not actually earning any interest income from their money invested.

How Long You Need to Hold I Savings Bonds?

These bonds are not actually designed to be traded as they are considered as long-term investments. Investors are not allowed to cash the bonds for at least one year after buying it. If the investors redeem these bonds before 5 years then they will be penalized for it and they need to pay 3 months interest to the issuer. So, invest smartly!

What are the Advantages of Series I Savings Bonds?

After EE and HH series bonds, another series of US savings bonds is the Series I bond. These bonds give protection with adequate returns. The risk of loss due to inflation is a major concern for investors. It can effect progressive investment very easily. But, these bonds give proper protection on their purchasing power too. You can by them through traditional and electronic mediums for safe and easy investment. The advantages of investing in these bonds are mentioned below-

1. **I series bonds don't include taxes**
   The first tax benefit of investing in **I savings bonds** is freedom from state and local taxes. As compared to other securities, these bonds are not subjected to any type of tax. The interest rate earned on monthly or annual basis is free from all sorts of taxes. Direct tax savings will boost your personal income very quickly and efficiently.
2. **The role of federal taxes**
   The next thing which you will get from **I savings bonds** is choice for payment of federal taxes. Just like EE series, this one also involves payment of federal taxes. This tax is paid on the interest earned while holding the bonds. It's mandatory for bondholders but the payment mechanism of this tax is beneficial for the bondholders. In this, the holders get two options for repayment. First is cash option and the second is accrual option. In first one, total tax is paid off at the time of redemption. Entire interest is paid off in one go. However, in second one, you get the option to pay interest on accrual basis. In this, you will pay the tax that is due on the interest you earned for the year that was added back to your principal. The flexibility in payment is a great benefit as sometimes people suffer a lot while paying their interest liabilities.
3. **The issuing range of these bonds**
   The benefit of these bonds is their issuing range. These bonds can issued at any amount between minimum and maximum limit. The minimum limit specified is $25 while the maximum is $10,000. Their holding period also varies from one to thirty years. The issuing range of these bonds can easily match the needs of small as well wealthy investors.

These were some advantages of investing in **I savings bonds**. These bonds can bring higher returns with full security of purchasing power. Your earnings can increase a lot by investing in these bonds.

Series HH

Series HH bonds have been discontinued. Unlike Series EE and I bonds, they do not increase in value, but pay interest every six months for 20 years. When they are cashed in or mature they are still worth face value. Issuance of Series HH bonds ended August 31, 2004.

From Wikipedia, the free encyclopedia, February 25, 2015, https://en.wikipedia.org/wiki/United_States_Treasury_security

Investment in Series HH Savings Bonds

HH savings bonds is one of the most popular and safe US savings bond. It is suitable for risk feared investors. In this, the issuing company gives a fixed return at regular intervals. They provide fixed rate of interest and are available on short as well as long term too. Institutional and soft term investors can benefit a lot through this savings bond.

1. **Profitability of these bonds- HH savings bonds** offer a fair deal of profit. Along with safety, they give efficient returns by avoiding market fluctuations and changes. The rate of interest is fixed which makes it profitable for small and conservative investors. The interest rate generated from these bonds is free from state and local income taxes. Thus, the amount of profits is further increased through the tax prospective of these bonds. But, they don't produce return on investment at maturity. Their redemption is conducted at face value only. All in all, these bonds can bring assured results without any hindrance or complication.

2. **The Interest Rate on these bonds-** The interest rate on **HH savings bonds** varies according to the time of repayment. For long term investment, the interest rates are better while for short term, the rates are much lower. Issuing companies fix the rate of interest according to ongoing market rates. They give fixed return and do not make any change until the maturity period is completed.

3. **Present availability of HH bonds-** Currently, **HH savings bonds** are not available for subscription. They were discontinued in 2004. You cannot exchange these bonds with EE series or other bonds. Reinvestment is also not possible with these bonds. But, the only option which can be considered is redemption. You can redeem these bonds for their face value. The interest rate of these bonds is stopped 20 years after completion of issuance. These bonds were an amazing option for easy, safe and fixed earning. They brought efficient results with least risk. Unavailability of such investment option is a major drawback for small investors. No other investment program from US government is providing such benefits with least risk of loss.

This was all about HH series bonds. These bonds have helped a lot in improving earning efficiency of people. Their fixed return and tax advantages have promoted institutional savings. Proper investment technique and market analysis were the main keys to achieve success while investing in these bonds.

Liberty bond

A Liberty Bond was a war bond that was sold in the United States to support the allied cause in World War I. Subscribing to the bonds became a symbol of patriotic duty in the United States and introduced the idea of financial securities to many citizens for the first time. The Act of Congress which authorized the Liberty Bonds is still used today as the authority under which all U.S. Treasury bonds are issued.

Securities, also known as Liberty Bonds, were issued in the aftermath of the September 11, 2001, terrorist attacks to finance the rebuilding of the areas affected.

There were four issues of Liberty Bonds:[2]

Apr 24, 1917 Emergency Loan Act authorizes issue of $5 billion in bonds at 3.5 percent.

Oct 1, 1917 Second Liberty Loan offers $3 billion in bonds at 3 percent

Apr 5, 1918 Third Liberty Loan offers $3 billion in bonds at 4.5 percent.

Sep 28, 1918 Fourth Liberty Loan offers $6 billion in bonds at 4.25 percent.

Interest on up to $30,000 in the bonds was tax exempt.

First Liberty Bond Act

The 1st Liberty Loan Act established a $5 billion aggregate limit on the amount of government bonds issued at 30 years at 3.5% interest, redeemable after 15 years. It raised $2 billion with 5.5 million people purchasing bonds.

Second Liberty Bond Act

The 2nd Liberty Loan Act established a $15 billion aggregate limit on the amount of government bonds issued, allowing $3 billion more offered at 25 years at 4% interest, redeemable after 10 years. The amount of the loan totaled $3.8 billion with 9.4 million people purchasing bonds.

Sales difficulties and the subsequent campaign

The response to the first Liberty Bond was unenthusiastic and although the $2 billion issue reportedly sold out, it probably had to be done below par because the notes traded consistently below par on the street. One reaction to this was to attack bond traders as "unpatriotic" if they sold below par. The Board of Governors of the New York Stock Exchange conducted an investigation of brokerage firms who sold below par to determine if "pro-German influences" were at work. The board forced one such broker to buy the bonds back at par and make a $100,000 donation to the Red Cross. Various explanations were offered for the weakness of the bonds ranging from German sabotage to the rich not buying the bonds because it would give an appearance of tax dodging (the bonds were exempt from some taxes).

First Service Star pamphlet

A common consensus was that more needed to be done to sell the bonds to small investors and the common man, rather than large concerns. The poor reception of the first issue resulted in a convertible re-issue five months later at the higher interest rate of 4% and with more favorable tax terms. Even so when the new issue arrived it also sold below par. This weakness continued with subsequent issues, the 4.25% bond priced as low as 94 cents upon arrival.

Secretary of the Treasury William Gibbs McAdoo reacted to the sales problems by creating an aggressive campaign to popularize the bonds. The government used famous artists to make posters, and used movie stars to host bond rallies. Al Jolson, Elsie Janis, Mary Pickford, Douglas Fairbanks and Charlie Chaplin were among the celebrities that made public appearances promoting the idea that purchasing a liberty bond was "the patriotic thing to do" during the era. Chaplin also made a short film, The Bond, at his own expense for the drive. Even the Boy Scouts and Girl Scouts sold the bonds, using the slogan "Every Scout to Save a Soldier". Beyond these effective efforts, in 1917 the Aviation Section of the U.S. Army Signal Corps established an elite group of Army pilots assigned to the Liberty Bond campaign. The plan for selling bonds was for the pilots to crisscross the country in their Curtis J4 "Jenny" training aircraft in flights of 3 to 5 aircraft. When they arrived over a town, they would perform acrobatic stunts, and put on mock dog fights for the populace.

After performing their air show, they would land on a road, a golf course, or a pasture nearby. By the time they shut down their engines, most of the townspeople, attracted by their performance, would have gathered. At that point, most people had never seen an airplane, and not ridden in one. Routinely each pilot stood in the rear cockpit of his craft and told the assemblage that every person who purchased a Liberty Bond would be taken for a ride in one of the airplanes. The program was successful in raising a substantial amount of money which was used to pay for the war effort. The methodology developed and practiced by the Army was later followed by numerous entrepreneurial flyers known as Barnstormers, who purchased war surplus Jenny airplanes and flew across the country selling airplane rides.

World War I poster. "Remember Belgium--Buy bonds--Fourth Liberty Loan" - During World War I, Allied Nations relied for propaganda on images and accounts of German atrocities to motivate their citizens to participate in the war effort. In this scene, the silhouetted German soldier with his thick Kaiser mustache drags a young girl away while the ruins of the city burn in the background.

1919 Victory Liberty Loan drive steel medallion made from "captured German cannon".

Vast amounts of promotional materials were manufactured. For example, for the third Liberty Loan 9 million posters, 5 million window stickers and 10 million buttons were produced and distributed.[10] The campaign spurred community efforts across the country and resulted in glowing, patriotically-tinged reports on the "success" of the bonds. For the fifth and final loan drive (the Victory Loan) in 1919 the Treasury Department produced steel medallions made from melted down German cannon that had been captured by American troops at Château-Thierry in NW France. The inch-and-a-quarter wide medallions suspended from a red, white, and blue ribbon were awarded by the Department to Victory Liberty Loan campaign volunteers in appreciation of their service in the drive.

Peak US indebtedness was in August 1919 at a value of $25,596,000,000 for Liberty Bonds, Victory Notes, War Savings Certificates, and other government securities. As early as 1922 the possibility that the war debt could not be paid in full within the expected schedule was raised, and that debt rescheduling may be needed. In 1921 the Treasury Department began issuing short term notes maturing in three to five years to repay the Victory Loan.

According to the Massachusetts Historical Society, "Because the First World War cost the federal government more than $30 billion (by way of comparison, total federal expenditures in 1913 were only $970 million), these programs became vital as a way to raise funds".

Despite all these measures, recent research has shown that patriotic motives played only a minor role in investors' decisions to buy these bonds;

Through the selling of "Liberty bonds," the government raised around $17 billion for the war effort. Considering that there were approximately 100 million Americans during that time, each American, on average, raised $170 on Liberty bonds.

Victory Liberty Loan

A fifth bond issue relating to World War I was released on April 21, 1919. Consisting of $4.5 billion of gold notes at 4.75% interest, they matured after 4 years but could be redeemed by the government after 3. Exempt from all income taxes, they were called at the time "the last of the series of five Liberty Loans." However they were also called the "Victory Liberty Loan," and appear this way on posters of the period.

Repayment

The first three bonds, and the Victory Loan, were partially retired during the course of the 1920s but the majority of these bonds were simply re-financed through other government securities. The Victory Loan, which was to mature in May 1923, was retired with money raised by short term treasury notes which matured after three to five years and issued at 90 day intervals until sufficient funds were raised in 1921. The likelihood of successfully retiring all of the war debt (within the amount of time) was noted as early as 1921.[12] In 1927, the 2nd and 3rd, together worth five billion dollars, 1/4 of all government debt at the time, were called for redemption and refunded through the issuance of other government securities through the Treasury Department. Some of the principal was retired. For example, of the 3.1 billion dollars owed on the 2nd Liberty Bond, 575 million in principal was retired and the rest refinanced. At this same time, the 1st Liberty Bond sill had 1.9 billion dollars outstanding in 1927 with a call date for 1932 while the fourth Liberty Bond, with six billion dollars, had a call date for 1932 as well.

Default of the Fourth Liberty Bond

 Wikimedia Commons has media related to Liberty bonds.

The first three Liberty bonds, and the Victory Loan, were retired during the course of the 1920s. However, because the terms of the bonds allowed them to be traded for the later bonds which had superior terms, most of the debt from the first, second, and third Liberty bonds was rolled into the fourth issue. As a result, the large majority of Liberty bond debt was still outstanding into the 1930s.

The fourth Liberty Bond had the following terms:

Date of Bond: October 24, 1918

Coupon Rate: 4.25%

Callable Starting: October 15, 1933

Maturity Date: October 15, 1938

Amount Originally Tendered: $6 billion

Amount Sold: $7 billion

The terms of the bond included: "The principal and interest hereof are payable in United States gold coin of the present standard of value."[18] This type of "gold clause" was common in both public and private contracts of the time, and was intended to guarantee that bond-holders would not be harmed by a devaluation of the currency.

However, when the US Treasury called the fourth bond on April 15, 1934,[18] it defaulted on this term by refusing to redeem the bond in gold, and neither did it account for the devaluation of the dollar from $20.67 per troy ounce of gold (the 1918 standard of value) to $35 per ounce. The 21 million bond holders therefore lost 139 million troy ounces of gold, or approximately 41% of the bond's principal. This was the equivalent of $2.866 billion (in 1918 dollars), or approximately $220 billion at the 2012 price of $1600 per ounce.

The legal basis for the refusal of the US Treasury to redeem in gold was House Joint Resolution 192, dated June 5, 1933.[19] The Supreme Court later held this to be unconstitutional under section 4 of the Fourteenth Amendment.:

We conclude that the Joint Resolution of June 5, 1933, insofar as it attempted to override the obligation created by the bond in suit, went beyond the congressional power.

Chief Justice Charles Evans Hughes, Perry v United States, 294 US 330 (1935), Page 294 U. S. 354

However, due to Roosevelt's elimination of the open gold market, the Court ruled that the bond-holders' loss was unquantifiable, and that to repay them in dollars according to the 1918 standard of value would be an "unjustified enrichment". The ruling therefore had little practical effect.

Chapter Eight
Convertible Bonds

The Facts you Should Know

Many novice players in investment arena often have a question in their mind, what are convertible bonds and whether they are stocks or bonds. Well, these are basically corporate bonds that are issued by corporations and organizations. It is totally different from other bond funds as it enables the bondholders to convert their bonds into common stock of the issuing corporation.

These bonds are usually converted into shares of stocks at a certain pre-announced ratio. Being a hybrid security, convertible bonds feature equity and debt like characteristics. Though this type of bond comes with lower coupon rate, but the bondholders are greatly compensated here because of the availability of shifting their normal bonds into shares of stock at a considerable rate of discount to market worth of the stocks.

When these bonds are issued they initially act a normal corporate bond with a little interest rate. Since, the bonds can be converted into stocks and bondholders can yield great benefits with the increasing price of the underlying stock, so the issuing corporations tend to provider lower yields against these convertibles. When the stock of the company performs weakly in the market then no conversion is allowed and hence the bondholders set stuck with the sub-par return of the bond.

Conversion Ratio

Conversion premium or conversion ratio basically finds out with each bond how many stocks or shares can be exchanged. This can also be expressed as the conversion rate or ratio and it is clearly mentioned in the agreement of the bond along with other provisions.

Forced Conversion

The major downfall of convertible bonds is that the issuing company at any time can forcibly convert the bonds. They have the right to call the bonds anytime. The forced conversion of bonds is basically done when the stock price is higher than the amount it would be if the bond were redeemed. Sometime forced conversion is also done at the call date of the bond. Due to this feature the actual capital appreciation potential of these bonds are restricted.

Conclusion

Overall, convertible bonds are mainly intended to offer a type of security blanket for all investors who wish to take part in the growth of a company. Remember, by investing in this type of bond you are simply restricting your downside risk at the disbursement of restricting your upside potential. But as a matter of fact, these bonds offer the investors with dual benefits of both equities as well as bonds.

. Essential Features Of Convertible Bonds

Convertible bonds are one of the most famous bonds of modern day period. These bonds can be converted into other securities during a particular period of time. They carry characteristics of fix income securities and are much better than other basic securities. The essential features of investing in these bonds are mentioned below-:

1. **Coupon Payment facility for investment**- The first feature of convertible bonds is the facility of coupon payments. These bonds have a coupon payment and are legally debt securities. Their value is calculated on the basis of prevailing interest rates and credibility of the issuer. The entire working of these bonds is just like traditional money market bonds.
2. **Exchange feature of the bond**- The next feature of convertible bond is easy exchange facility. This feature of a convertible bond gives the right to the holder to

covert the par value of the bond into common shares at a specified price or conversion rate. A bond of $1000 can be converted into specified amount of shares at a fixed rate of conversion. This rate can vary according to different market rates.

3. **Premium for a convertible issue**- Premium for a convertible transaction will be the difference between the price at which convertible bond is available for purchase in the open market and intrinsic value of the issue's. It can be calculated on currency as well as percentage too.

4. **Limited downside risk with these bonds**- An essential benefit from **convertible bonds** is limited downside risks. Unlike owning a company's stock whose price could fall to $0, holders of convertible bonds are promised the par value of the bond at maturity regardless of the stock price. This reduces the risk of loss in an easy and efficient manner.

5. **A chance for higher earning**- The next benefit of **convertible bonds** is chances of higher earnings. As compared to traditional bonds, convertible bond holders can have maximum benefits from increasing stock prices by converting the bond into shares of common stock when the original price is much higher than the conversion rate.

These were some features of investing in **convertible bonds**. These bonds give an efficient way to earn more with fewer complications. They have a place in various diversified portfolios due to their dual quality which combines debt and equity features. The valuation of these bonds is bit complicated but proper efforts definitely bring higher returns.

Convertible bond

In finance, a convertible bond or convertible note (or a convertible debenture if it has a maturity of greater than 10 years) is a type of bond that the holder can convert into a specified number of shares of common stock in the issuing company or cash of equal value. It is a hybrid security with debt- and equity-like features. It originated in the mid-19th century, and was used by early speculators such as Jacob

Little and Daniel Drew to counter market cornering. Convertible bonds are most often issued by companies with a low credit rating and high growth potential.

To compensate for having additional value through the option to convert the bond to stock, a convertible bond typically has a coupon rate lower than that of similar, non-convertible debt. The investor receives the potential upside of conversion into equity while protecting downside with cash flow from the coupon payments and the return of principal upon maturity. These properties lead naturally to the idea of convertible arbitrage, where a long position in the convertible bond is balanced by a short position in the underlying equity.

From the issuer's perspective, the key benefit of raising money by selling convertible bonds is a reduced cash interest payment. The advantage for companies of issuing convertible bonds is that, if the bonds are converted to stocks, companies' debt vanishes. However, in exchange for the benefit of reduced interest payments, the value of shareholder's equity is reduced due to the stock dilution expected when bondholders convert their bonds into new shares.

Types

The underwriters have been quite innovative and provided various variations of the initial convertible structure. Although no clear classification formally exists in the financial market it is possible to segment the convertible universe into the following sub-types:

Vanilla convertible bonds are the most plain convertible structures. They grant the holder the right to convert into certain amount of shares determined according to a conversion price determined in advance. They may offer coupon regular payments during the life of the security and have a fixed maturity date where the nominal value of the bond is redeemable by the holder. This type is the most common convertible type and is typically providing the asymmetric returns profile and positive convexity often wrongly associated to the entire asset class: at maturity the holder would indeed either convert into shares or request the redemption at par depending on whether or not the stock price is above the conversion price.

Mandatory convertibles are a common variation of the vanilla subtype, especially on the US market. Mandatory convertible would force the holder to convert into shares at maturity - hence the term "Mandatory". Those securities would very often bear two conversion prices, making their profiles similar to a "risk reversal" option strategy. The first conversion price would limit the price where the investor would receive the equivalent of its par value back in shares, the second would delimit where the investor will earn more than par. Note that if the stock price is below the first conversion price the investor would suffer a capital loss compared to its original investment (excluding the potential coupon payments). Mandatory convertibles can be compared to forward selling of equity at a premium.

Reverse convertibles are a less common variation, mostly issued synthetically. They would be opposite of the vanilla structure: the conversion price would act as a knock-in short call option: as the stock price drops below the conversion price the investor would start to be exposed the underlying stock performance and no longer able to redeem at par its bond. This negative convexity would be compensated by a usually high regular coupon payment.

Packaged convertibles or sometimes "Bond + Option" structures are simply a straight bonds and a call option/warrant wrapped together. Usually the investor would be able to then trade both legs separately. Although the initial payoff is similar to a plain vanilla one, the Packaged Convertibles would then have different dynamics and risks associated with them since at maturity the holder would not receive some cash or shares but some cash and potentially some share. They would for instance miss the modified duration mitigation effect usual with plain vanilla convertibles structures.

Additional features

Any convertible bond structure, on top of its type, would bear a certain range of additional features as defined in its issuance prospectus:

Conversion price: The nominal price per share at which conversion takes place, this number is fixed at the issuance but could be adjusted under some circumstance described in the issuance prospectus (e.g. underlying stock split). You could have more than one conversion price for non-vanilla convertible issuances.

Issuance premium: Difference between the conversion price and the stock price at the issuance.

Conversion ratio: The number of shares each convertible bond converts into. It may be expressed per bond or on a per centum (per 100) basis.

Maturity/redemption date: Final payment date of a loan or other financial instrument, at which point the principal (and all remaining interest) is due to be paid. In some cases, there is no maturity date (i.e. perpetual), this is often the case with preferred convertibles (e.g. US0605056821).

Final conversion date: Final date at which the holder can request the conversion into shares. Might be different from the redemption date.

Coupon: Periodic interest payment paid to the convertible bond holder from the issuer. Could be fixed or variable or equal to zero.

Yield: Yield of the convertible bond at the issuance date, could be different from the coupon value if the bond is offering a premium redemption. In those cases the yield value would determine the premium redemption value and intermediary put redemption value.

Convertibles could bear other more technical features depending on the issuer needs:

Call features: The ability of the issuer (on some bonds) to call a bond early for redemption. This should not be mistaken for a call option. A Softcall would refer to a call feature where the issuer can only call under certain circumstances, typically based on the underlying stock price performance (e.g. current stock price is above 130% of the conversion price for 20 days out of 30 days). A Hardcall feature would not need any specific conditions beyond a date: that case the issuer would be able to recall a portion or the totally of the issuance at the Call price (typically par) after a specific date.

Put features: The ability of the holder of the bond (the lender) to force the issuer (the borrower) to repay the loan at a date earlier than the maturity. These often occur as windows of opportunity, every three or five years and allow the holders to exercise their right to an early repayment.

Contingent conversion (aka CoCo): Restrict the ability of the convertible bondholders to convert into equities. Typically, restrictions would be based on the underlying stock price and/or time (e.g. convertible every quarter if stock price is above 115% of the conversion price).[2] Reverse convertibles in that respect could be seen as a variation of a Mandatory bearing a contingent conversion feature based. More recently some CoCo's issuances have been based on Tier-1 capital ratio for some large bank issuers.

Reset: Conversion price would be reset to a new value depending on the underlying stock performance. Typically, would be in cases of underperformance (e.g. if stock price after a year is below 50% of the conversion price the new conversion price would be the current stock price).

Change of control event (aka Ratchet): Conversion price would be readjusted in case of a take-over on the underlying company. There are many subtype of ratchet formula (e.g. Make-whole base, time dependent...), their impact for the bondholder could be small (e.g. ClubMed, 2013) to significant (e.g. Aegis, 2012). Often, this clause would grant as well the ability for the convertible bondholders to "put" i.e. ask for the early repayment of their bonds.

Uses for issuers

Lower fixed-rate borrowing costs. Convertible bonds allow issuers to issue debt at a lower cost. Typically, a convertible bond at issue yields 1% to 3% less than straight bonds.

Locking into low fixed–rate long-term borrowing. For a finance director watching the trend in interest rates, there is an attraction in trying to catch the lowest point in the cycle to fund with fixed rate debt, or swap variable rate bank borrowings for fixed rate convertible borrowing. Even if the fixed market turns, it may still be possible for a company to borrow via a convertible carrying a lower coupon than ever would have been possible with straight debt funding.

Higher conversion price than a rights issue strike price. Similarly, the conversion price a company fixes on a convertible can be higher than the level that the share price ever reached recently. Compare the equity dilution on a convertible issued on, say, a 20 or 30pct premium to the higher equity dilution on a rights issue, when the new shares are offered on, say, a 15 to 20pct discount to the prevailing share price.

Voting dilution deferred. With a convertible bond, dilution of the voting rights of existing shareholders only happens on eventual conversion of the bond. However convertible preference shares typically carry voting rights when preference dividends are in arrears. Of course, the bigger voting impact occurs if the issuer decides to issue an exchangeable rather than a convertible.

Increasing the total level of debt gearing. Convertibles can be used to increase the total amount of debt a company has in issue. The market tends to expect that a company will not increase straight debt beyond certain limits, without it negatively impacting upon the credit rating and the cost of debt. Convertibles can provide additional funding when the straight debt "window" may not be open. Subordination of convertible debt is often regarded as an acceptable risk by investors if the conversion rights are attractive by way of compensation.

Maximizing funding permitted under pre-emption rules. For countries, such as the UK, where companies are subject to limits on the number of shares that can be offered to non-shareholders non-pre-emptively, convertibles can raise more money than via equity issues. Under the UK's 1989 Guidelines issued by the Investor Protection Committees (IPCs) of the Association of British Insurers (ABI) and the National Association of Pension Fund Managers (NAPF), the IPCs will advise their members not to object to non-pre-emptive issues which add no more than 5pct to historic non-diluted balance sheet equity in the period from AGM to AGM, and no more than 7.5pct in total over a period of 3 financial years. The pre-emption limits are calculated on the assumption of 100pct probability of conversion, using the figure of undiluted historic balance sheet share capital (where there is assumed a 0pct probability of conversion). There is no attempt to assign probabilities of conversion in both circumstances, which would result in bigger convertible issues being permitted. The reason for his inconsistency may lie in the fact that the Pre Emption Guidelines were drawn up in 1989, and binomial evaluations were not commonplace amongst professional investors until 1991-92.

Premium redemption convertibles such as the majority of French convertibles and zero-coupon Liquid Yield Option Notes (LYONs), provide a fixed interest return at issue which is significantly (or completely) accounted for by the appreciation to the redemption price. If, however, the bonds are converted by investors before the maturity date, the issuer will have benefited by having issued the bonds on a low or even zero-coupon. The higher the premium redemption price, (1) the more the shares have to travel for conversion to take place before the maturity date, and (2) the lower the conversion premium has to be at issue to ensure that the conversion rights are credible.

Takeover paper. Convertibles have a place as the currency used in takeovers. The bidder can offer a higher income on a convertible than the dividend yield on a bid victim's shares, without having to raise the dividend yield on all the bidder's shares. This eases the process for a bidder with low-yield shares acquiring a company with higher-yielding shares. Perversely, the lower the yield on the bidder's shares, the easier it is for the bidder to create a higher conversion premium on the convertible, with consequent benefits for the mathematics of the takeover. In the 1980s, UK domestic convertibles accounted for about 80pct of the European convertibles market, and over 80pct of these were issued either as takeover currency or as funding for takeovers. They had several cosmetic attractions.

The pro-forma fully diluted earnings per share shows none of the extra cost of servicing the convertible up to the conversion day irrespective of whether the coupon was 10pct or 15pct. The fully diluted earnings per share is also calculated on a smaller number of shares than if equity was used as the takeover currency. In some countries (such as Finland) convertibles of various structures may be treated as equity by the local accounting profession. In such circumstances, the accounting treatment may result in less pro-forma debt than if straight debt was used as takeover currency or to fund an acquisition. The perception was that gearing was less with a convertible than if straight debt was used instead. In the UK the predecessor to the International Accounting Standards Board (IASB) put a stop to treating convertible preference shares as equity. Instead it has to be classified both as (1) preference capital and as (2) convertible as well. Nevertheless, none of the (possibly substantial) preference dividend cost incurred when servicing a convertible preference share is visible in the pro-forma consolidated pretax profits statement. The cosmetic benefits in (1) reported pro-forma diluted earnings per share, (2) debt gearing (for a while) and (3) pro-forma consolidated pre-tax profits (for convertible preference shares) led to UK convertible preference shares being the largest European class of convertibles in the early 1980s, until the tighter terms achievable on Euroconvertible bonds resulted in Euroconvertible new issues eclipsing domestic convertibles (including convertible preference shares) from the mid-1980s.Tax advantages. The market for convertibles is primarily pitched towards the non-taxpaying investor. The price will substantially reflect (1) the value of the underlying shares, (2) the discounted gross income advantage of the convertible over the underlying shares, plus (3) some figure for the embedded optionality of the bond. The tax advantage is greatest with mandatory convertibles. Effectively a high tax-paying shareholder can benefit from the company securitizing gross future income on the convertible, income which it can offset against taxable profits.

From Wikipedia, the free encyclopedia, February 25, 2015
https://en.wikipedia.org/wiki/Convertible_bond

Chapter Nine
Junk Bonds

Junk Bonds High-yield debt

In finance, a high-yield bond (non-investment-grade bond, speculative-grade bond, or junk bond) is a bond that is rated below investment grade. These bonds have a higher risk of default or other adverse credit events, but typically pay higher yields than better quality bonds in order to make them attractive to investors. Sometimes the company can provide new bonds as a part of yield which can only be redeemed after its expiry or maturity.

Risk

The holder of any debt is subject to interest rate risk and credit risk, inflationary risk, currency risk, duration risk, convexity risk, repayment of principal risk, streaming income risk, liquidity risk, default risk, maturity risk, reinvestment risk, market risk, political risk, and taxation adjustment risk. Interest rate risk refers to the risk of the market value of a bond changing due to changes in the structure or level of interest rates or credit spreads or risk premiums. The credit risk of a high-yield bond refers to the probability and probable loss upon a credit event (i.e., the obligor defaults on scheduled payments or files for bankruptcy, or the bond is restructured), or a credit quality change is issued by a rating agency including Fitch, Moody's, or Standard & Poors.

A credit rating agency attempts to describe the risk with a credit rating such as AAA. In North America, the five major agencies are Standard and Poor's, Moody's, Fitch Ratings, Dominion Bond Rating Service and A.M. Best. Bonds in other countries may be rated by US rating agencies or by local credit rating agencies. Rating scales vary; the most popular scale uses (in order of increasing risk) ratings of AAA, AA, A, BBB, BB, B, CCC, CC, C, with the additional rating D for debt already in arrears. Government bonds and bonds issued by government-sponsored enterprises (GSEs) are often considered to be in a zero-risk category above AAA; and categories like AA and A may sometimes be split into finer subdivisions like "AA−" or "AA+".

Bonds rated BBB− and higher are called investment grade bonds. Bonds rated lower than investment grade on their date of issue are called speculative grade bonds, or colloquially as "junk" bonds.

The lower-rated debt typically offers a higher yield, making speculative bonds attractive investment vehicles for certain types of portfolios and strategies. Many pension funds and other investors (banks, insurance companies), however, are prohibited in their by-laws from investing in bonds which have ratings below a particular level. As a result, the lower-rated securities have a different investor base than investment-grade bonds.

The value of speculative bonds is affected to a higher degree than investment grade bonds by the possibility of default. For example, in a recession interest rates may drop, and the drop in interest rates tends to increase the value of investment grade bonds; however, a recession tends to increase the possibility of default in speculative-grade bonds.

Extracted from www February 25 2015 at
https://en.wikipedia.org/w/index.php?title=High-yield_debt&action=edit&section=1

Corporate debt

The original speculative grade bonds were bonds that once had been investment grade at time of issue, but where the credit rating of the issuer had slipped and the possibility of default increased significantly. These bonds are called "fallen angels".

The investment banker Michael Milken realized that fallen angels had regularly been valued less than what they were worth. His time with speculative grade bonds started with his investment in these. Only later did he and other investment bankers at Drexel Burnham Lambert, followed by those of competing firms, begin organizing the issue of bonds that were speculative grade from the start. Speculative grade bonds thus became ubiquitous in the 1980s as a financing mechanism in mergers and acquisitions. In a leveraged buyout (LBO) an acquirer would issue speculative grade bonds to help pay for an acquisition and then use the target's cash flow to help pay the debt over time.

In 2005, over 80% of the principal amount of high-yield debt issued by U.S. companies went toward corporate purposes rather than acquisitions or buyouts.[1]

In emerging markets, such as China and Vietnam, bonds have become increasingly important as term financing options, since access to traditional bank credits has always been proved to be limited, especially if borrowers are non-state corporates. The corporate bond market has been developing in line with the general trend of capital market, and equity market in particular.[2]

Extracted from www February 25, 2015 at https://en.wikipedia.org/w/index.php?title=High-yield_debt&action=edit&section=3

Debt repackaging and subprime crisis

High-yield bonds can also be repackaged into collateralized debt obligations (CDO), thereby raising the credit rating of the senior tranches above the rating of the original debt. The senior tranches of high-yield CDOs can thus meet the minimum credit rating requirements of pension funds and other institutional investors despite the significant risk in the original high-yield debt.

 The New York City headquarters of Barclays (formerly Lehman Brothers, as shown in the picture). In background, the AXA Center, headquarters of AXA, first worldwide insurance company.

When such CDOs are backed by assets of dubious value, such as subprime mortgage loans, and lose market liquidity, the bonds and their derivatives become what is referred to as "toxic debt". Holding such "toxic" assets has led to the demise of several investment banks such as Lehman Brothers and other financial institutions during the subprime mortgage crisis of 2007–09 and led the US Treasury to seek congressional appropriations to buy those assets in September 2008 to prevent a systemic crisis of the banks.[3]

Such assets represent a serious problem for purchasers because of their complexity. Having been repackaged perhaps several times, it is difficult and time-consuming for auditors and accountants to determine their true value. As the recession of 2008–09 bites, their value is decreasing further as more debtors default, so they represent a rapidly depreciating asset. Even those assets that might have gone up in value in the long-term are now depreciating rapidly, quickly becoming "toxic" for the banks that hold them.[4] Toxic assets, by increasing the variance of banks' assets, can turn otherwise healthy institutions into zombies. Potentially insolvent banks have made too few good loans creating a debt overhang problem.[5] Alternatively, potentially insolvent banks with toxic assets will seek out very risky speculative loans to shift risk onto their depositors and other creditors.[6]

On March 23, 2009, U.S. Treasury Secretary Timothy Geithner announced a Public-Private Investment Partnership (PPIP) to buy toxic assets from banks' balance sheets. The major stock market indexes in the United States rallied on the day of the announcement rising by over six percent with the shares of bank stocks leading the way.[7] PPIP has two primary programs. The Legacy Loans Program will attempt to buy residential loans from banks' balance sheets. The Federal Deposit Insurance Corporation will provide non-recourse loan guarantees for up to 85 percent of the purchase price of legacy loans. Private sector asset managers and the U.S. Treasury will provide the remaining assets. The second program is called the legacy securities program which will buy mortgage backed securities (RMBS) that were originally rated AAA and commercial mortgage-backed securities (CMBS) and asset-backed securities (ABS) which are rated AAA. The funds will come in many instances in equal parts from the U.S. Treasury's Troubled Asset Relief Program monies, private investors, and from loans from the Federal Reserve's Term Asset Lending Facility (TALF). The initial size of the Public Private Investment Partnership is projected to be $500 billion.[8] Nobel Prize–winning economist Paul Krugman has been very critical of this program arguing the non-recourse loans lead to a hidden subsidy that will be split by asset managers, banks' shareholders and creditors.[9] Banking analyst Meredith Whitney argues that banks will not sell bad assets at fair market values because they are reluctant to take asset write downs.[10] Removing toxic assets would also reduce the volatility of banks' stock prices. Because stock is akin to a call option on a firm's assets, this lost volatility will hurt the stock price of distressed banks. Therefore, such banks will only sell toxic assets at above market prices.[11]

Extracted from www February 25, 2015 at
https://en.wikipedia.org/w/index.php?title=High-yield_debt&action=edit&section=4

High-yield bond indices

High-yield bond indices exist for dedicated investors in the market. Indices for the broad high-yield market include the S&P U.S. Issued High Yield Corporate Bond Index (SPUSCHY), CSFB High Yield II Index (CSHY), Citigroup US High-Yield Market Index, the Merrill Lynch High Yield Master II (H0A0), the Barclays High Yield Index, and the Bear Stearns High Yield Index (BSIX). Some investors, preferring to dedicate themselves to higher-rated and less-risky investments, use an index that only includes BB-rated and B-rated securities, such as the Merrill Lynch Global High Yield BB-B Rated Index (HW40). Other investors focus on the lowest quality debt rated CCC or distressed securities, commonly defined as those yielding 1500 basis points over equivalent government bonds.

Chapter Ten
Insurance bond

An insurance bond (or investment bond) is a single premium life assurance policy for the purposes of investment. Due to tax laws they are a common form of investment in the UK and some offshore centers. Traditionally insurance bonds were with-profits policies and were often called with-profit(s) bonds. Since the introduction of unitised insurance funds they have often been marketed as unit-linked bonds or investment bonds.

Why invest in an insurance bond?

The decision of which 'wrapper' to place funds within (i.e. onshore bond, offshore bond or collective) can be complex and is based upon the tax position of the investor, the treatment of each wrapper, the likely growth and investment term.

Insurance bonds can be useful vehicles for minimizing tax as they do not incur the 50% CGT reduction on assets held for 12 months or more.

Useful features of Bonds for tax planning scenarios include the tax deferred status, the ability to write the investment in trust and reduce the inheritance tax liability on an estate, and exclusive access to expensive investment links like guaranteed or protected profits funds are to name a few. Bonds can provide income or growth and when income is required there are now bonds that can offer a set minimum guaranteed income for life of the plan holder.

For UK Financial Advisers, the Financial Services Authority is placing increasing focus on what wrapper is being recommended. Advisers must be able to demonstrate they have used a robust process when selecting a bond or collective.

From Wikipedia, the free encyclopedia February 25, 2015
https://en.wikipedia.org/wiki/Insurance_bond

Chapter Eleven
Zero-coupon bond

A zero-coupon bond (also discount bond or deep discount bond) is a bond bought at a price lower than its face value, with the face value repaid at the time of maturity.[1] Note that this definition assumes a positive time value of money. It does not make periodic interest payments, or have so-called "coupons", hence the term zero-coupon bond. When the bond reaches maturity, its investor receives its par (or face) value. Examples of zero-coupon bonds include U.S. Treasury bills, U.S. savings bonds, long-term zero-coupon bonds, and any type of coupon bond that has been stripped of its coupons.

In contrast, an investor who has a regular bond receives income from coupon payments, which are made semi-annually or annually. The investor also receives the principal or face value of the investment when the bond matures.

Some zero coupon bonds are inflation indexed, so the amount of money that will be paid to the bond holder is calculated to have a set amount of purchasing power rather than a set amount of money, but the majority of zero coupon bonds pay a set amount of money known as the face value of the bond.

Zero coupon bonds may be long or short term investments. Long-term zero coupon maturity dates typically start at ten to fifteen years. The bonds can be held until maturity or sold on secondary bond markets. Short-term zero coupon bonds generally have maturities of less than one year and are called bills. The U.S. Treasury bill market is the most active and liquid debt market in the world.

Strip bonds

Zero coupon bonds have a duration equal to the bond's time to maturity, which makes them sensitive to any changes in the interest rates. Investment banks or dealers may separate coupons from the principal of coupon bonds, which is known as the residue, so that different investors may receive the principal and each of the coupon payments. This creates a supply of new zero coupon bonds.

The coupons and residue are sold separately to investors. Each of these investments then pays a single lump sum. This method of creating zero coupon bonds is known as stripping and the contracts are known as strip bonds. "STRIPS" stands for Separate Trading of Registered Interest and Principal Securities.

Dealers normally purchase a block of high-quality and non-callable bonds—often government issues—to create strip bonds. A strip bond has no reinvestment risk because the payment to the investor occurs only at maturity.

The impact of interest rate fluctuations on strip bonds, known as the bond duration, is higher than for a coupon bond. A zero coupon bond always has a duration equal to its maturity; a coupon bond always has a lower duration. Strip bonds are normally available from investment dealers maturing at terms up to 30 years. For some Canadian bonds the maturity may be over 90 years.

In Canada, investors may purchase packages of strip bonds, so that the cash flows are tailored to meet their needs in a single security. These packages may consist of a combination of interest (coupon) and/or principal strips.

In New Zealand, bonds are stripped first into two pieces—the coupons and the principal. The coupons may be traded as a unit or further subdivided into the individual payment dates.

In most countries, strip bonds are primarily administered by a central bank or central securities depository. An alternative form is to use a custodian bank or trust company to hold the underlying security and a transfer agent/registrar to track ownership in the strip bonds and to administer the program. Physically created strip bonds (where the coupons are physically clipped and then traded separately) were created in the early days of stripping in Canada and the U.S., but have virtually disappeared due to the high costs and risks associated with them.

Uses

Pension funds and insurance companies like to own long maturity zero-coupon bonds because of the bonds' high duration. This high duration means that these bonds' prices are particularly sensitive to changes in the interest rate, and therefore offset, or immunize the interest rate risk of these firms' long-term liabilities.

Taxes

In the United States, a zero-coupon bond would have Original issue discount (OID) for tax purposes. Instruments issued with OID generally impute the receipt of interest (sometimes called phantom income), even though these bonds don't pay periodic interest. Because of this, zero coupon bonds subject to U.S. taxation should generally be held in tax-deferred retirement accounts, to avoid paying taxes on future income. Alternatively, when purchasing a zero coupon bond issued by a U.S. state or local government entity, the imputed interest is free of U.S. federal taxes, and in most cases, state and local taxes, too.

Zero coupon bonds were first introduced in 1960s, but they did not become popular until the 1980s. The use of these instruments was aided by an anomaly in the US tax system, which allowed for deduction of the discount on bonds relative to their par value. This rule ignored the compounding of interest, and led to significant tax-savings when the interest is high or the security has long maturity. Although the tax loopholes were closed quickly, the bonds themselves are desirable because of their simplicity.

In India, the tax on income from deep discount bonds can arise in two ways: interest or capital gains. It is also law that interest has to be shown on accrual basis for deep discount bonds issued after February 2002. This is as per CBDT circular No 2 of 2002 dated 15 February 2002.

From Wikipedia, the free encyclopedia, February 25, 2015

Chapter Twelve
Treasury Securities

Treasury Securities & Programs

U.S. Treasury securities are a great way to invest and save for the future. Here, you'll find overviews regarding U.S. Treasury bonds, notes, bills, TIPS, and Floating Rate Notes (FRNs), as well as U.S. Savings Bonds.

Treasury Securities

Here's what's available:

Treasury Bills

Treasury bills are short-term government securities with maturities ranging from a few days to 52 weeks. Bills are sold at a discount from their face value. Treasury bills, or T-bills, are sold in terms ranging from a few days to 52 weeks. Bills are typically sold at a discount from the par amount (also called face value). For instance, you might pay $990 for a $1,000 bill. When the bill matures, you would be paid $1,000. The difference between the purchase price and face value is interest. It is possible for a bill auction to result in a price equal to par, which means that Treasury will issue and redeem the securities at par value.

Use Treasury bills to:

•Diversify your investment portfolio

•Participate in a secure, short-term investment

Treasury Bills in Depth

Treasury bills, or T-bills, are typically issued at a discount from the par amount (also called face value). For example, if you buy a $1,000 bill at a price per $100 of $99.986111, then you would pay $999.86 ($1,000 x .99986111 = $999.86111).* When the bill matures, you would be paid its face value, $1,000. Your interest is the face value minus the purchase price. It is possible for a bill auction to result in a price equal to par, which means that Treasury will issue and redeem the securities at par value.

You can bid for a bill in two ways:

- With a **noncompetitive bid**, you agree to accept the discount rate determined at auction. With this bid, you are guaranteed to receive the bill you want, and in the full amount you want.

- With a **competitive bid**, you specify the discount rate you are willing to accept. Your bid may be: 1) accepted in the full amount you want if the rate you specify is less than the discount rate set by the auction, 2) accepted in less than the full amount you want if your bid is equal to the high discount rate, or 3) rejected if the rate you specify is higher than the discount rate set at the auction.

To place a noncompetitive bid, you may use TreasuryDirect, or a bank or broker.

To place a competitive bid, you must use a bank or broker.

Key Facts:

- Bills are sold at a discount. The discount rate is determined at auction.

- Bills pay interest only at maturity. The interest is equal to the face value minus the purchase price.

- Bills are sold in increments of $100. The minimum purchase is $100.

- All bills except 52-week bills and cash management bills are auctioned every week. The 52-week bill is auctioned every four weeks. Cash management bills aren't auctioned on a regular schedule.

- Cash management bills are issued in variable terms, usually only a matter of days.

- Bills are issued in electronic form.

- You can hold a bill until it matures or sell it before it matures.

- In a single auction, a bidder can buy up to $5 million in bills by non-competitive bidding or up to 35% of the initial offering amount by competitive bidding.

*Treasury rounds to the nearest penny using conventional mathematical rounding methods.

Treasury Bills: How to Buy

You can buy Treasury bills directly from the U.S. Treasury or through a bank, broker, or dealer.

The table below shows the types of bills available for purchase by both means.

Term	TreasuryDirect	Bank/or Broker
4-Week Bill	Yes	Yes
13-Week Bill	Yes	Yes
26-Week Bill	Yes	Yes
52-Week Bill	Yes	Yes
Cash Management Bills	No	Yes

You can bid for a bill in two ways:

- With a **noncompetitive bid**, you agree to accept the discount rate determined at auction. With this bid, you are guaranteed to receive the bill you want, and in the full amount you want.

- With a **competitive bid**, you specify the discount rate you are willing to accept. Your bid may be: 1) accepted in the full amount you want if the rate you specify is less than the discount rate set by the auction, 2) accepted in less than the full amount you want if your bid is equal to the high discount rate, or 3) rejected if the rate you specify is higher than the discount rate set at the auction.

To place a noncompetitive bid, you may use TreasuryDirect, or a bank or broker.

To place a competitive bid, you must use a bank or broker.

*Treasury rounds to the nearest penny using conventional mathematical rounding methods.

Extracted from the www, February 22, 2015,

Treasury Notes

Treasury notes are government securities that are issued with maturities of 2, 3, 5, 7, and 10 years and pay interest every six months. Treasury notes, sometimes called T-Notes, earn a fixed rate of interest every six months until maturity. Notes are issued in terms of 2, 3, 5, 7, and 10 years. You can buy notes from us in TreasuryDirect. You also can buy them through a bank or broker.

Treasury notes, or T-notes, are issued in terms of 2, 3, 5, 7, and 10 years, and pay interest every six months until they mature.

The price of a note may be greater than, less than, or equal to the face value of the note. For a full discussion of the price of a note, see Treasury Notes: Rates and Terms.

When a note matures, you are paid its face value.

Notes are sold in TreasuryDirect, and by banks and brokers. You can bid for a note in either of two ways:

- With a **noncompetitive bid**, you agree to accept the yield determined at auction. With this bid, you are guaranteed to receive the note you want, and in the full amount you want.

- With a **competitive bid**, you specify the yield you are willing to accept. Your bid may be: 1) accepted in the full amount you want if your bid is less than the yield determined at auction, 2) accepted in less than the full amount you want if your bid is equal to the high yield, or 3) rejected if the yield you specify is higher than the yield set at auction.

To place a noncompetitive bid, you may use TreasuryDirect, a bank, or a broker.

To place a competitive bid, you must use a bank or broker.

Key Facts

- The yield on a note is determined at auction.

- Notes are sold in increments of $100. The minimum purchase is $100.

- Notes are issued in electronic form.

- You can hold a note until it matures or sell it before it matures.

- In a single auction, a bidder can buy up to $5 million in notes by non-competitive bidding or up to 35% of the initial offering amount by competitive bidding.

Extracted from the www February 22, 2015 at http://www.treasurydirect.gov/indiv/research/indepth/tnotes/res_tnote.htm

Treasury Bonds

Treasury bonds pay interest every six months and mature in 30 years. Treasury bonds pay a fixed rate of interest every six months until they mature. They are issued in a term of 30 years. You can buy Treasury bonds from us in TreasuryDirect. You also can buy them through a bank or broker.

Treasury Inflation-Protected Securities (TIPS)

TIPS are marketable securities whose principal is adjusted by changes in the Consumer Price Index. TIPS pay interest every six months and are issued with maturities of 5, 10, and 30 years. Treasury Inflation-Protected Securities, or TIPS, provide protection against inflation. The principal of a TIPS increases with inflation and decreases with deflation, as measured by the Consumer Price Index. When a TIPS matures, you are paid the adjusted principal or original principal, whichever is greater. TIPS pay interest twice a year, at a fixed rate. The rate is applied to the adjusted principal; so, like the principal, interest payments rise with inflation and fall with deflation. You can buy TIPS from us in TreasuryDirect. You also can buy TIPS through a bank or broker.

How TIPS Are Tied to Inflation

Treasury Inflation-Protected Securities (TIPS) are marketable securities whose principal is adjusted by changes in the Consumer Price Index. With inflation (a rise in the index), the principal increases. With a deflation (a drop in the index), the principal decreases.

The relationship between TIPS and the Consumer Price Index affects both the sum you are paid when your TIPS matures and the amount of interest that a TIPS pays you every six months. TIPS pay interest at a fixed rate. Because the rate is applied to the adjusted principal, however, interest payments can vary in amount from one period to the next. If inflation occurs, the interest payment increases. In the event of deflation, the interest payment decreases.

At the maturity of a TIPS, you receive the adjusted principal or the original principal, whichever is greater. This provision protects you against deflation.

Treasury provides TIPS Inflation Index Ratios to allow you to easily calculate the change to principal resulting from changes in the Consumer Price Index. To learn more about determining how inflation adjustments affect your security, please see TIPS: Rates and Terms.

Methods of Buying TIPS

TIPS are sold in TreasuryDirect, and through banks and brokers. **NOTE:** TIPS no longer are sold in Legacy Treasury Direct, which is being phased out.

The price of a TIPS can be less than, equal to, or greater than the face value. For a full discussion of the price of a TIPS, see TIPS: Rates and Terms.

You can bid for TIPS in either of two ways:

- With a **noncompetitive bid**, you agree to accept the yield determined at auction. With this bid, you are guaranteed to receive the TIPS you want, and in the full amount you want.

- With a **competitive bid**, you specify the yield you are willing to accept. Your bid may be: 1) accepted in the full amount you want if your bid is less than the yield determined at auction, 2) accepted in less than the full amount you want if your bid is equal to the high yield, or 3) rejected if the yield you specify is higher than the yield set at auction.

To place a noncompetitive bid, you may use TreasuryDirect, a bank, or a broker.

To place a competitive bid, you must use a bank or broker.

Key Facts:

- TIPS are issued in terms of 5, 10, and 30 years.

- The interest rate on a TIPS is determined at auction.

- TIPS are sold in increments of $100. The minimum purchase is $100.

- TIPS are issued in electronic form.

- You can hold a TIPS until it matures or sell it in the secondary market before it matures.

- In a single auction, a bidder can buy up to $5 million in TIPS by non-competitive bidding or up to 35% of the initial offering amount by competitive bidding.

Extracted from the www February 22, 2015 at http://www.treasurydirect.gov/indiv/research/indepth/tips/res_tips.htm

Interest payments from Treasury Inflation-Protected Securities (TIPS), and increases in the principal of TIPS, are

Floating Rate Notes (FRNs)

Interest payments on an FRN rise and fall based on discount rates for 13-week Treasury bills. FRNs are issued for a term of 2 years and pay interest quarterly. The U.S. Treasury began issuing Floating Rate Notes (FRNs) in January 2014. Issued for a term of two years, FRNs pay varying amounts of interest quarterly until maturity. Interest payments rise and fall based on discount rates in auctions of 13-week Treasury bills. We offer FRNs in TreasuryDirect and through banks and brokers. Once you purchase an FRN, you can hold it until it matures or sell it before it matures.

FRNs In Depth

The U.S. Treasury began issuing Floating Rate Notes (FRNs) in January 2014. The securities have a term of two years.

The price of an FRN may be greater than, less than, or equal to the face value of the security.

When an FRN matures, you are paid its face value.

FRNs are sold in TreasuryDirect and by banks and brokers. You can bid for an FRN in either of two ways:

- With a noncompetitive bid, you agree to accept the high discount margin determined at auction. With this bid, you are guaranteed to receive the FRN you want, and in the full amount you want.

- With a competitive bid, you specify the discount margin you are willing to accept. Your bid will be: 1) accepted in the full amount you want if your bid is less than the high discount margin determined at auction, 2) accepted in less than the full amount you want if your bid is equal to the high discount margin, or 3) rejected if your bid is above the high discount margin.

To place a noncompetitive bid, you may use TreasuryDirect, a bank, or a broker.

To place a competitive bid, you must use a bank or broker.

Results of recent FRN auctions

Key Facts

- Interest payments on FRNs rise and fall, based on discount rates for 13-week bills.

- FRNs are sold in increments of $100. The minimum purchase is $100.

- FRNs are issued in electronic form.

- You can hold an FRN until it matures or sell it before it matures.

- In a single auction, a bidder can buy up to $5 million in FRNs by non-competitive bidding or up to 35% of the initial offering amount by competitive bidding.

Extracted from the www February 22, 2015 at http://www.treasurydirect.gov/indiv/research/indepth/frns/res_frn.htm

I Savings Bonds

I Savings Bonds are a low-risk savings product that earn interest while protecting you from inflation. Sold at face value. Series I Savings Bonds are a low-risk, liquid savings product. While you own them they earn interest and protect you from inflation. You may purchase I Bonds via TreasuryDirect or with your IRS tax refund. As a TreasuryDirect account holder, you can purchase, manage, and redeem I Bonds directly from your Web browser.

EE and E Savings Bonds

EE and E Savings Bonds are a secure savings product that pay interest based on current market rates for up to 30 years. Electronic EE Savings Bonds are sold at face value in TreasuryDirect. Series EE savings bonds are safe, low-risk savings products that pay interest based on current market rates for up to 30 years for bonds purchased May 1997 through April 30, 2005*. You may purchase EE Bonds via TreasuryDirect. As a TreasuryDirect account holder, you can purchase, manage, and redeem EE Bonds directly from your Web browser.

Treasury bonds are issued in terms of 30 years and pay interest every six months until they mature. When a Treasury bond matures, you are paid its face value.

The price and yield of a Treasury bond are determined at auction. The price may be greater than, less than, or equal to the face value of the bond. For more on the price of a Treasury bond, see Treasury Bonds: Rates and Terms.

Treasury bonds are sold in TreasuryDirect (but not in Legacy Treasury Direct, which is being phased out) and by banks and brokers.

Two types of bids are accepted:

- With a **noncompetitive bid**, you agree to accept the interest rate determined at auction. With this bid, you are guaranteed to receive the bond you want, and in the full amount you want.

- With a **competitive bid**, you specify the yield you are willing to accept. Your bid may be: 1) accepted in the full amount you want if your bid is equal to or less than the yield determined at auction, 2) accepted in less than the full amount you want if your bid is equal to the high yield, or 3) rejected if the yield you specify is higher than the yield set at auction.

To place a noncompetitive bid, you may use TreasuryDirect, a bank, or a broker.

To place a competitive bid, you must use a bank or broker.

Bonds exist in either of two formats: as paper certificates (these are older bonds) or as electronic entries in accounts. Today we issue Treasury bonds in electronic form, not paper. Paper Treasury bonds can be converted to electronic form (see instructions below).

Paper Treasury Bonds

To contact us for information on paper Treasury bonds:

- Send us an e-mail

- Call us at 304-480-7711

- Write to:
  Bureau of the Public Debt
  P.O. Box 426
  Parkersburg, WV 26106-0426

Key Facts

- The yield on a bond is determined at auction.

- Bonds are sold in increments of $100. The minimum purchase is $100.

- You can hold a Treasury bond until it matures or sell it before it matures.

- In a single auction, a bidder can buy up to $5 million in bonds by non-competitive bidding or up to 35% of the initial offering amount by competitive bidding.

Extracted from the www February 22, 2015 at http://www.treasurydirect.gov/indiv/research/indepth/tbonds/res_tbond.htm

Treasury Securities That Have Stopped Earning Interest

Do you have savings bonds that have matured and stopped earning interest? If so, it's time to cash them in, or reinvest them, and have your money start working for you again.

It's important to check your savings bonds periodically to determine if they're still earning interest, and if they're not, they should be redeemed. Use the tables below to determine whether your bonds have stopped earning interest, or for how long you can expect them to earn interest. (You should keep a list of your bonds, by serial number, in a safe location and separate from the actual bonds.)

You can also check Treasury Hunt, if you're not sure whether you own any bonds that have matured. This system provides information only and doesn't give you status of your bonds. For status, you need to contact:

- Bureau of the Fiscal Service
  P.O. Box 2186
  Parkersburg, WV 26106-2186

Also, marketable securities are subject to bond calls, cases where the Treasury stops paying interest on bonds before the scheduled maturity date. Be sure to note your security's maturity date and check the website for bond calls.

NOTE: Marketable securities - U. S. Treasury bills, notes, bonds, Floating Rate Notes, and Treasury Inflation-Protected Securities (TIPS) - have maturities ranging from a few days to 30 years.

The following savings bonds no longer earn interest:

SERIES	ISSUE DATE
E	All issues
EE	January 1980 through February 1985
H	All issues
HH	January 1980 through February 1995
Savings Notes	All issues
A, B, C, D, F, G, J, K	All issues

How long savings bonds earn interest, based on issue date:

SERIES	ISSUE DATE	NUMBER OF YEARS BONDS EARN INTEREST
E	May 1941- November 1965	40 years
	December 1965 - June 1980	30 years
EE	All issues	30 years
H	June 1952- January 1957	29 years, 8 months
	February 1957- December 1979	30 years
HH	All issues	20 years
I	All issues	30 years
Savings Notes	All issues	30 years

Extracted from www, February 22, 2015,
http://www.treasurydirect.gov/indiv/research/securities/res_securities_stoppedearninginterest.htm

Chapter Thirteen

Stock, Mutual Fund or Bond Investment Clubs

These clubs normally buy stocks, mutual funds or bonds. Prior to 2008 many of these type of clubs existed in major cities and were disbanded as they incurred significant losses from changes in the economy. Members and club owners were typically unsophisticated investors making investment decisions based on biased advertising paid for by the same companies who were seeking additional capital. Typical members have very little knowledge of: fundamental analysis, technical analysis, call and put options, financial analysis, and value investing to make wise investment decisions consistently. Club owners and members are not normally required to hold a securities license as long as they refrain from soliciting compensation in exchange for financial advice or soliciting the sale of stock, mutual funds or bonds in third party companies. One allowed exception is that a CEO / President or CFO of a C Corporation is allowed to solicit stock or bonds in their corporation as long as they provide a private placement memorandum that complies with the law to their new shareholders. One additional requirement is that non-accredited investors must be Directors of the C Corporation in addition to being shareholders.

Extracted from www February 25, 2015 at https://en.wikipedia.org/w/index.php?title=Investment_club&action=edit&section=5

Legal structure

Investment clubs are generally formed as general partnerships, but could also be formed as limited liability companies, limited liability partnerships, corporations, or sole proprietorship that transfer real estate assets to a group living trust (similar to a family trust). While an investment club could incorporate, the double tax treatment on corporate distributions makes the corporate structure less desirable than a partnership except in the case when a C Corporation pays out qualified dividends after deducting allowable expenses. Typically, a general partnership does not generate any tax liability on its own; instead, any tax liability is passed through to members each year. However, income taxes are generally much higher than taxes on qualified dividends.

In order to understand the legal structure that an investment club should choose, the club should first understand its club type. Each of the different club types will have different legal requirements as well as different reporting requirements. Typically, the SEC only requires reporting for investment groups with over 100 members, which is reclassified as an investment group, not an investment club. Publicly held offerings like a Real Estate Investment Trust as known as a REIT also have additional reporting requirements.

Extracted from www February 25, 2015 at
https://en.wikipedia.org/w/index.php?title=Investment_club&action=edit&section=10

Tax implications

In the United States Investment club partnerships must file Form 1065 and Schedule K-1s with the IRS each year, and with states that require partnership filings.[citation needed] In the United Kingdom investment clubs and their members are required to submit form 185(new) to HMRC each year.[citation needed] Investment club accounting software can facilitate the management of a club's books and the preparation of tax filings.

Extracted from the www February 25, 2015 at
https://en.wikipedia.org/w/index.php?title=Investment_club&action=edit&section=11

Chapter Fourteen
Commercial Paper

A Short Guide

In global financial marketplace, commercial paper plays a very crucial role. This is an unsecured promissory note that is issued by corporations with a predetermined maturity period which is not more than 270 days. It is also considered as a money market security that is sold or issued by corporations and large organizations with an aim to get funds from buyers to meet their short term debt obligations, like payrolls etc.

Commercial paper is basically backed by issuing corporation and bank's guarantees to pay off the exact face value of the note at the time of maturity period which is mentioned in the note. This note is not actually supported by any collateral bodies; thereby organizations and corporations with exceptional credit ratings are allowed to sell this commercial paper at public marketplace at very affordable rates. They are actually issued by corporations at a discount from actual face value and it promises higher interest repayment rates than all other bond funds available today. Usually, the longer the period of maturity of commercial note, the higher the interest rate you can get from the corporations against your note. However, the interest rates of commercial notes also fluctuate according to the market trends, but they are quite lower compared to the rates of banks.

Rates and Pricing

The current rates that you need to pay against the commercial paper can be seen on the official website of The Federal Reserve Board. FRB also responsible for publishing the rates of non-financial and AA rated financial commercial paper and they publish it on H.15 Statistical Release every Monday around 2.30pm. FRB makes use of a data for publishing the rates and the data is taken from DTCC (Depository Trust & Clearing Corporation). The rates are first estimated by the experts on the basis of expected relationship between maturities of coupon and the rates of new issues.

One can get the figures of outstanding issued commercial papers which are usually available at the closing of business every Wednesday and also at the last business day of each month.

Benefits of Using A Commercial Paper

Commercial paper is a popular short term money market instrument. It's a debt instrument which is valid for nine months or less. A short term **commercial paper** is available in several forms. It can be a promissory note, US Treasury bill and certificate of deposit. The essential benefits of using this money market instrument are given below-

- **Liquidity, the most essential benefit**- Today, large companies and government agencies use commercial papers to fill gaps of cash flow. Private companies can also issue short term instruments to cover the time between performing work and receiving payment. This reduces the requirement of keeping cash reserves for future expenses. Thus, business expansion projects are conducted efficiently through this paper.

- **A quick and cost effective way**- **Commercial paper** offers an easy way to raise capital. As compared to other money market instruments, **commercial paper** offers a better and efficient way to raise capital. You can conduct your business very easily by raising money through a commercial paper or US Treasury bill.

- **Affordable for general public**- The next benefit of commercial paper is affordability. As compared to bank loans, commercial papers are much cheaper and reliable. Small investors can buy them for catering their short term financial needs. Their low price point is an amazing attraction for short term investors.

- **Return of investment without any commitment**- The next benefit of commercial paper is return on investment. This monetary instrument offers return on investment without long term commitment from the borrowers. This makes it an essential option for small institutional investors who want to save more with less investment. However, the rate of return may depend on the type of instrument and the terms decided by the company.

- **Availability of an exit option**- The last benefit of commercial paper is presence of an exit option. If you want to close your investment then there is always an option with commercial paper. Commercial papers are issued with the option to quit investment. You can close them anytime by following predefined rules and regulations.

These were some essential benefits of commercial papers. This monetary instrument is an essential option for short term investment. It can give higher returns without creating any issue. Therefore, if you want to earn more with less investment then consider commercial paper as viable option. It will give you many benefits at a reasonable price value.

Conclusion

Today, commercial paper is increasingly becoming available for all retail investors and they can easily purchase it from several authorized outlets. Investors who are looking for higher yields will definitely find this note very interesting; owing to the higher returns it offers that too with modest risks. You may contact your financial advisor for more information on commercial paper.

Chapter Fifteen

Importance of Credit Rating Agencies

A credit rating agency is an agency which assigns credit ratings to various financial institutions and companies issuing stocks, bonds and other financial securities. It gives an idea of creditworthiness of a borrowing firm or corporation. Through these agencies, an investor can analyze the volume of risk while investing his money. Some factors which explain the importance of credit rating agencies are-

1. **Protection against the risk of bankruptcy**- The first factor which enhances the value of credit rating agencies is protection against bankruptcy. The agency gives an idea about the degree of financial strength of the issuer company. It gives a fair idea about which company is good and which one is bad. Thus, investors can make most from their money without financial loss or bankruptcy.

2. **Recognition of financial and other risks**- An efficient credit rating agency also gives an idea of financial other investment risks. The symbols offered by the agency gives an idea to continue the investment in an easy and efficient way. They not only give a better view of risks but also conduct a safe and profitable investment.

3. **A sense of efficiency**- An efficient credit rating agency saves the work of company analysis. The concern of company's performance, management and efficiency is eliminated with a reliable agency. The trained and experienced professionals from an efficient agency handle all the work efficiently. Their detailed analysis report can save your efforts very easily. They will give a detailed report of the company which you are targeting.

4. **Easy to understand**- Another benefit from a credit rating agency is easy understandability. The process of understanding the ratings is very simple and easy. You don't need any professional or analytical skills to understand the report. You can take instant decisions about any security of the company.

5. **Elimination of intermediaries**- These days, market investors hire professional experts for seeking advice on various investments. They hire intermediaries due to lack of professional knowledge and experience. But, presence of credit rating symbols can give a fair idea for investment. They can not only save your money but can also assure better from the investments.

These were some factors which explain the importance of credit rating agencies. An efficient agency acts as a perfect guide for investment. It gives an idea of creditability and promotes safe and effective investment. These agencies follow some standards and give best of their efforts to conduct perfect analysis.

A Brief History of all the Rating Agencies

Credit ratings play a very important role in the financial game. It offers institutional and individual investors with all the required information that helps them to determine whether the issuing body of fixed income securities and debt obligations will be able to meet the obligations in regards to those securities. The rating agencies are highly dedicated in offering the investors with the objective analyses and independent assessment of countries and companies that mainly issue such securities or bonds. There are mainly three rating agencies – Fitch Ratings, Moody's Investors Service and Standard & Poor's. Below you will come across with the functions and evolution of these rating agencies.

Fitch Ratings

In 1913, The Fitch Publishing Company was established under the dynamic leadership of John Knowles Fitch. This organization first published the financial statistics through "The Fitch Stock and Bond Manual" and it was intended to be used in investment industry. Through a system of D Rating, the Fitch introduced the AAA Ratings in the year 1924 and soon it became the basic of ratings across the investment industry. With an aim to emerge as a full-fledge global rating agency, The Fitch merged with IBCA of London in the year 1990. In early 2004, the company also launched some operation subsidiaries that specialize in data services, enterprise risk management and finance industry training.

Moody's Investors Service

In 1900, the John Moody & Company first published its "Moody Manual". This manual comprises basic statistics and some other general information about different bonds and stocks of different industries. Till the time the stock market crashed in 1907 this manual was the only national publication. Later in the year 1909, the company again published Moody's Analyses of Railroad Investments which comprises details of different securities and its value. With an aim to expand this idea, the company established a division called Moody's Investors Services in 1914 and the prime focus of this division is to offer ratings to almost all government bonds available in the market. In early 70s, Moody's Investors Service also started rating the commercial paper and other bank deposits, thus making it a full-service rating agency which is globally recognized today.

Standard & Poor's

In the year 1860, The History of Railroads and Canals in United States was first published by Henry Varnum Poor, which was the predecessor of securities analysis and reporting. In 1906, the Standard Statistics was formed to publish sovereign debt, corporate bonds, and some municipal bond ratings. In the year 1914, the Poor's Publishing merged with the Standard Statistics and hence the Standard and Poor's Corporation was formed. Today, this rating agency is globally recognized for its indexes like S&P 500, which is a stock market index and act both as a tool for decision making and investor analysis and economic indicator for USA.

Sixteen
Earnings and Inventory

Why are Earnings Important to you as an Investor?

You can never be a successful investing in the stock market without having a thorough understanding of earnings. Every industry place in the stock market is often infatuated with earnings and what significance they have. So, why do earnings draw so much focus? In order to understand the significance of earnings to investors and any other individual involved in the stock market, it is important to understand what earnings are.

Definition of Earnings: In simple terms, company's earnings are profits obtained in a given financial period. For instance, when a company sells a product, the revenue obtained minus all the costs and expenses, gives you the earning.

Earnings Per Share: In an attempt to get the earnings of various companies, both investors as well as analysts rely on a ratio know as EPS (Earnings per share). EPS is calculated by picking the earnings left over to be distributed amongst shareholders and dividing by the total number of shares outstanding. Many investors and analysts describe earnings using the EPS ratio. Since every company has its own amount of shares belonging to the public, taking into account only the company's earnings doesn't give an accurate reflection of how much cash every firm made from its shares. Because of this, EPS is used to draw comparisons which are valid.

Earnings Season: In the stock market, this season resembles a school report card where all publicly traded companies in the U.S. are supposed to make their financial reports public. This happens on a quarterly basis (4 times a year) in accordance to the law. It is worth mentioning that while some firms opt to use the normal calendar year for reporting purposes, others have their own fiscal calendars for financial reporting.

Despite the fact that investors look forward to seeing a firm's financial returns, the earnings per share (EPS) is the most critical figure that attracts a lot of media attention and analysis from industry stakeholders. Prior to the official earnings reports being released, stock analysts begin speculating and issue rough estimates of what they think will be released. These financial forecasts are often compiled by a consortium of various financial research and analysis firms.

When a firm surpasses this estimate, it is referred to as an earnings surprise and this causes stock prices to go higher. If the earnings come below expectations, the price is said to disappoint and the prices move lower.

How are Earnings important for an investor?

The main reason why investors are always preoccupied with company earnings is because they ultimately drive stock prices. It's important to note that earnings directly affect the prices of stocks. Strong earnings cause stock prices to appreciate while a reduction causes stock prices to drop. Rising prices imply that investors are optimistic that the company will perform well in the future.

Companies with high earnings always cause excitement and anticipation amongst investors and everyone wants to reap the potential benefits. The internet boom is an example of how high performing companies were able to attract a high number of investors. After some time, it became evident that investors weren't going to make as much money as they had hoped because for some firms, it became impossible for the market to keep up with the high valuations without any support from earnings. This eventually led to a fall in stock prices.

When a company wants to make money, there are two techniques it can use. First is to make substantial improvements to available products and come up with new ones. Alternatively, a firm can pass funds to its shareholders either in form of a share buyback or a dividend. Remember, in the case of dividends, you get your money right away but for share buyback, the money is reinvested in the company for development projects. Typically, smaller companies concentrate on reinvesting profits in order to build a share holder value while on the other hand, large firms opt to pay out dividends. There is no technique that has an advantage over the other, they both have a long term goal which is to create a higher earnings potential which in turn, enables shareholders to earn a return on their investment.

In summary, earnings simply mean profits that a firm realizes. EPS (Earnings per share) is a key earnings indicator that sheds light into a company's financial health. Wall Street keeps a close eye on earnings reports and as an investor, staying informed about earnings is the best way to determine whether your investment will provide you with a solid return. This means that for every investor, anything to do with earnings especially for a company you have invested in is critical information for you. Knowing the meaning of terminologies such as EPS can save you a lot of stress when interpreting company earnings.

How Do You Use Earnings Information to Make an Investment Decision?

Before making any investment decision, it is important to have your facts right before making a good decision. In each financial quarter, publicly-traded firms are obliged to the make their earnings public in order to report performance. Using earnings report, both current and prospective investors have a good idea of the financial health of a company they wish to invest in. Financial breakdowns such as EPS (earnings per share), sales, expenses and net income is critical information for investment. For those who wish to invest, current and potential investors can use present earnings reports and compare them with previous ones.

There several techniques investors can use to analyze an earnings report. A simple and really easy way is to compare the actual reported figures versus what was anticipated before the results were results. Prior to the announcement of a company's earnings, advance polls are carried out and analysts are asked to give their views on what they are expecting. As an investor, you should be following these events clearly because they will give you a heads-up on what to expect. It's worth mentioning that once the polling has been done, the media picks the averages and sends out the forecasts to members of the public. On the other hand, the market also gives its own forecast depending on the stock price. For an investor, this process is critical because it helps you to have a good idea of what is happening in a company.

Immediately the earnings report becomes public, the market begins to experience elaborate movements. In the event that the results released are better than expected, the net profits are higher and this makes the stock prices of a company to increase rapidly. Alternatively, when earnings are announced after the markets have closed, the stock opening prices for the following day will be high. It is important for any investor to understand and have this information at their fingertips for the purposes of making sound investment decisions.

When the year draws to a close, a lot of companies begin to release the earnings reports. At this juncture, both traders and investors are on the lookout to either sell or buy their stocks depending on whether the officially announced earnings figures turn out to be better or worse than what analysts estimated. It is good to know that the actual figures released indeed have an immediate impact on the stocks and understanding the consequences of earnings reports on a stock price is the best approach to make good investment decisions.

As an investor, you should look at a firm's net profit and make comparisons with the anticipated figures to determine if a firm surpassed analyst expectations. Since its common knowledge that an earnings report has immense influence on stock prices, it is up to investors to learn how to manipulate this information for their benefit. Every investor should know that any move in stock prices as result of a firm's earnings is an important event that cannot be ignored.

So, how can an investor benefit from this knowledge? In most cases, markets never accurately price stocks in response to recently released earnings reports. This means that a smart investor should look for opportunities which can enable them to come up with wiser investment decisions. Some of the good indicators to watch out for include;

- A scenario whereby an earnings report is more positive than the analysts expected but surprisingly, stock prices fail to increase as anticipated is a perfect opportunity for investors to think of a buy in.
- An earnings report comes out slightly higher than expected but stock prices rise too high above what was expected. In this case, an investor should contemplate to short-sell.
- A stock earnings report performs dismally, worse than analysts expected, but contrary to expectations, the stock price takes a positive turn. This could be a perfect short-sell scenario.

The good news is that there are several ways an investor can use to their advantage during the earnings season. The key aspect here is to understand the consequences of an earnings report and what impact it has on stock prices. With all these knowledge, an investor has the knowledge to trade and quickly respond to opportunities as they come.

What Does Value Investing Mean?

Everyone who has an interest in the stock market must have heard of the term value investing. But what exactly does it mean? Value investing refers to the procedure of choosing stocks that are priced and trade less than their real value. A value investor usually preoccupies themselves with choosing stocks whose price-to-book or price-to-earnings ratio is lower than the average. It's important to note that doing this is not as simple as it sounds because there are complexities and must knows that are involved.

If you are interesting in long term investments, value investing is a key aspect that you need to think about. Investors who pay attention to value investing are able to comfortably withstand the numerous challenges that come with stock investing and are more likely to emerge victorious compared to those who ride the market. Value investing focuses on getting higher profits while spending the least money because the reason for value is to have profits. Value investing is an investment technique that works well for good stocks at great prices as compared to great stocks at good prices.

You should know that value investing doesn't focus on how much a stock price has risen or fallen. Rather, a lot of focus in placed in the intrinsic value and whether a stock is presently trading below the real value i.e. at a discount. It is important to note that when choosing overpriced stocks, the only hope one has is that the price of the stock will continue to gain value based on future events because it has already represented a company's worth. On the other hand, undervalued stocks are often sold at a discount and therefore, unforeseen events don't really have an impact because even if there are no extra earnings or additional profits, the shares are already expected to go back to their original inherent value.

A question that many people ask is "why would stock prices fail to reflect their true and intrinsic value of their shares?" in summary, value investors believe that share prices are never accurate when referenced to the underlying value of shares and their company. The market theory suggests that share prices are always a true reflection of everything an investor needs to know about a company a theory that value investors disagree with.

An important question to answer is "Can shares be bought for less than their actual value?" Before answering this question, you would want to first know how an intrinsic value is accurately determined. It is good to note that firms are always either overvalued or undervalued regardless of how the overall markets are performing.

As an investor, you should brace yourself of frequent market volatility and other challenges associated with stock investing. A lot of industry experts have said before that if as an investor you are not prepared to take a 50% value decline, investing is certainly not the right venture for you. This is because one has to suffer a significant amount of losses before the market begins to experience gains. Value investors are not interested in timing the market before they can invest. Actually, they are more focused with underlying company fundamentals as a more critical consideration prior to investing.

Value investors believe in the quality of a company they are investing in and a lot of their screening techniques are long term. They also look for look for less volatile environment and therefore, are less susceptible to market panic compared to the average investors.

In order to be a successful value investor, you must learn how to strike the balance. On one hand, you don't have to be worried about market depressions, recoveries and upturns since your investment was made based on the underlying quality of the value of the investment.

On the other hand, investments should only be undertaken in firms which are reputable and have the potential to succeed in any environment. For value investors, it is important to do thorough investment research and making wise investment decisions. Value investors feel this is a better approach than trying so hard to forecast the markets in order to find a suitable stock to invest in. Value investing has enabled several entrepreneurs such as Warren Buffett to acquire huge amounts of wealth.

How do I Use Fundamental Analysis to make an Investment Decision?

Fundamental analysis is a critical process that facilitates an investor to carefully analyze a company before making any key investment decisions. Using this approach, it is possible to analyze a company by examining various aspects such as market competition, management structure and current standing of a company in the market. Thanks to comprehensive fundamental analysis, investors have been able to make sound and informed financial decisions because they understand the workings of a company they are interested to invest in.

It's worth mentioning that the surrounding political climate has immense impact on the growth and operations of a company. Unstable governments and tense political environments are known to propagate tension which leads to anxiety and insecurity. While there are some factors that promote corporate growth and development, others hinder growth and therefore, it is good for every investor to keep their eyes on the ground and closely watch both political and economical developments.

Understanding the cycle of the industry is critical prior to making any investment decisions. Initial phase, growth, maturity and decline are all part of an industry life cycle and this information is of great benefit to both existing and prospective investors. A careful study of the industry helps an investor to deeply understand various industry phases and how to take the appropriate action.

Company analysis is an in-depth analysis of a company's financial performance, management, annual reports as well as ratios. The integrity and caliber of company managers, their ratings and performance are all critical issues to take into account. Annual reports are useful because they help an investor to ascertain the financial viability of a company. The annual report includes information such as financial statements, Schedules as well as both the director's and auditor's reports.

Using the director's report, it is possible to get the views and opinions of the director on general industry issues and the performance of a company. Furthermore, information on current and future projects as well as expansion plans is included in the director's report. On the other hand, the auditor's report gives details on the accounting principles used and the results of any changes that have been effected.

Critical financial documents such as Profit and Loss statement and balance sheets are critical pointers of a company's financial performance. The financial statements should also give an account of a firm's assets, liabilities, profit and loss and other related activities that have taken place within a specified accounting period. In addition, the effects that are likely to come as a result of the financial statements need to be clearly understood.

Before making any investment decisions, it is essential to analyze liquidity ratio, profitability ratio and market value ratio amongst other financial indicators to understand a firm's financial background. The market value ratio reflects the period when an investor makes a move to purchase stocks until the time it takes for them to recoup their investment. The profitability ratio on the other hand, gives details of the total assets and returns on equity. Using these metrics, it makes it simple for an investor to learn about how a company is performing in the industry. Asset management ratio gives a breakdown of how assets are managed while liquidity management enables the investor to ascertain whether a firm will be able to live up to its financial obligations.

The intrinsic share value changes frequently as a result of both internal and external factors. Having good knowledge in this area makes it easy for an investor to invest wisely. This should be regardless of whether an investor is new or they are increasing the number of shares purchased. Even though fundamental analysis is a comprehensive and challenging task, it is wise for every investor to learn how to use fundamentals to get a clearer picture of the company as well as its performance which directly impacts the level of investment.

A lot of investors have been able to make good decisions thanks to fundamental analysis. Investors should know that putting money in a new venture is not an overnight decision but rather a key decision that should only be taken after careful consideration of all the information involved.

What is Ratio Analysis?

There's a lot more to financial statements than most of us think. Financial analysts are always working around the clock to unlock the secrets behind these numbers. The whole idea of doing ratio analysis is to determine if a company is performing better or worse than the previous years and how it is coping with market competition. It is worth mentioning that making comparisons between competitors can be challenging especially when numbers are used.

In this case, using ratios is better because this is a more standardized approach where financial statements are standardized and some of the critical figures expressed as ratios and percentages. For instance, balance sheet positions are expressed as a percentage of the total assets, a percentage of total sales are reflected in income statement positions while a sum of total sources of cash or total uses of cash are expressed as cash flow positions.

In addition, getting good results from financial statements should be to come up with a base year that will be used as a reference point. Next, changes in percentage points should be used to reflect any changes. Financial ratios are based on a simple concept; two numbers picked from financial statements, divided them and name the result. Because of this, there are a large number of ratios which are divided into the following categories;

Liquidity measures: This ratio refers to the capability of a company to honor its bills.

Profitability measures: The level of efficiency that a company uses to manage and oversee its operations.

Asset management measures: This is a measure of the capability a company has to utilize its assets in order to generate revenue.

Market value measures: Is the stock price a true representation of the value of a company?

Liquidity measures: The best and most widely used ratios are the current ratio which is current assets divided by current liabilities as well as the Quick or Acid-Test ratio computed by current assets-inventory divided by current liabilities. Note that the higher the value of the ratio, the higher the chances a company has to meet its obligations. The Acid Test ratio takes into account the inventory might be challenging to sell and hence it is excluded from the ratio.

The total debt ratio (Total assets- total equity) divided by the total assets addresses the long term viability of a company. However, if debt is utilized well, a company can be able to manage it assets and in turn, obtain higher profits.

Asset Management measures: Inventory Turnover and Day Sales inventory is computed as the inventory turnover which is obtained by cost of goods sold divided by the inventory. The resultant value Days' sales in inventory is obtained with the formula 365 days/inventory turnover. This value indicates on average how many days an inventory stays before it is sold. Similarly, Receivables Turnover is the helps you to understand the timespan within which a company will collect on its receivables.

Profitability Measures: This helps both investors and analysts to understand how much profit a corporation has obtained for every $ sold. Profitability measure is obtained by dividing the Net income by Sales. Despite the fact that everyone loves an increased profit margin, there are firms which have succeeded immensely by reducing their selling prices and achieving more sales at a lower margin. ROA (Return on Assets) indicates how investor assets have contributed to realizing profits. ROE (Return on Equity) is obtained by Net Income/Total Equity and gives details of how much cash was obtained thanks to the amount shareholders put into the basis.

Market Value Measures: Here, we have P/E Price Earnings Ratio which means price per share/earnings per share and is a widely used ratio. The dot com era however, has overvalued stock with a point where the P/E rose to a high of 32 when traditionally, it is known to revolve around 15%. The important point to note is that a PE of 0-10 is an indication of an undervaluation of a company. On the other hand, a PE of 17 and above indicates a company stock is overvalued.

Ratio analysis is an important concept because it is the only accurate way to portray a company's true financial reflection.

As earlier mentioned, comparing numbers of different companies is an uphill task and doesn't guarantee the best results. For instance, the only way to know if a company has been undervalued or overvalued is to know how to calculate and interpret ratios.

Factors such as geographical location also influence the ratios but it has been challenging for analysts and industry players to pinpoint the reasons. However, the use of mathematics to determine a firm's real value is assuring because you're guaranteed of accurate values that can be depended upon to make critical decisions. Understanding the role of ratio analysis and how it can benefit you as an investor or trader is essential for successful trading.

What are Assets?

If you are interested in financial and money matters, it is important for you to understand the different types of terminologies used. An asset is any item with value which can be converted into cash. Ownership of assets is far and wide and spans from governments, business enterprises as well as individuals. This is a common term that is used in the business sector and is used as an important parameter for the preparation of various financial statements. Some common examples of assets include; personal property which is anything that belongs to you as an individual.

Items such as furniture, cars, jewelry, and collectibles among others can be classified as personal property. However, it is important to mention that there are some assets such as furniture, cars that belong to businesses and organizations. Cash and its equivalents are also classified as assets and examples include; treasury bills, physical cash, checking and savings accounts, certificates of deposit among others. Real estate property such as land, buildings or any structures that are located on a piece of land owned either by an individual or an organization. Another common type of assets is investments which include retirement plans, pensions, life insurance policies, annuities, bonds, cash value of life insurance policies among other investments.

Assets are divided into two broad categories which are liquid assets and illiquid assets. A liquid assets is one which is easily and quickly converted into cash without undergoing a lot of effort. For example, assets such as stocks, government bonds and other market instruments are liquid assets. On the other hand, illiquid assets cannot be easily converted into cash and involve some procedures before the sale is finalized. Assets such as land, antiques, cars and other collectibles fall under the category of illiquid assets.

Your net worth is determined by subtracting your liabilities from your assets. In summary, assets are all items that belong to you while liabilities are things you owe others. When you have a positive net worth, it means you have more assets than liabilities which is a good thing. On the other hand, a negative net worth signifies your liabilities exceed your assets.

Interestingly, assets can also be classified either as tangible assets or intangible assets. Tangible assets are those that take a physical form and include buildings, cars and furniture among others. On the other hand, intangible assets take the form of a concept and don't have a physical representation. Some of the assets classified as intangible include trade or brand names, domain names among others. It's important to note that despite the fact that there are several categories of assets, a lot of people focus their attention on the following;

Cash: Cash assets consist of paper money, checks, money orders payable to the business are examples of assets.

Accounts Receivable: This is whereby a business sells products or services to its clients on credit. Despite the fact that no immediate exchange of cash is involved, there is an outstanding amount that should be paid to the business in future.

Inventory: This refers to the raw materials that are used to manufacture goods and goods in stock that have not yet been put on sale.

Supplies: A lot of items fall under this category and they include boxes, blades, pens, paper, stamps, printer toners, tapes and labels among other office stationery. It's essential to mention that most of the office stationery is usually utilized within a year.

Prepaid expenses: This refers to a scenario whereby a business pays for its expenses before their due date. These advance payments are meant to offset expenses in good time to enable a business to carry on with its activities in a smooth manner.

Equipment and property: Assets such buildings, land and other key assets such as machinery that belong to an organization fall under this category.

In order to clearly understand assets and the value they have in a business, it is important to have a good idea of the classification of assets. This way, you can be able to easily know what is relevant for you and how you can classify either your personal or business assets. Remember that the more assets you have, the better you're financially and chances are high your financial score cards will be good.

What are Accounts Receivable?

Accounts receivable is a common term that is used in business circles. It refers to the amount of money that customers owe a business after goods have been supplied to them on credit. Accounts receivable is also known as trade receivable which is reflected on the balance sheet under the current assets category since this amount is treated as debt related. Anyone who has the intentions of venturing into business should be familiar with the various accounting terms and practices that are applied within the industry. Accounts receivable is one of the many transactions that any successful business enterprise has to deal with.

It is extremely crucial for an enterprise to effectively manage working capital and keep track of cash flow to ensure it meets the liquidity needs of a business. Advancements in accounts receivable technologies have come into existence in the recent times to facilitate for quick, accurate and simpler processing of day-to-day transactions. There are several reasons why a business needs to have accounts receivable services and they include;

-Reconciliation of customer accounts
-Achieve better cash flow with faster customer settlement
-Centrally managed invoice control
-Banking of customer receipts
-On time generation of customer invoices

Businesses have the option to deal with accounts receivable services in-house or find a professional bookkeeping company and outsource this service to them. Using well trained expert professionals is the best way to guarantee that a good job will be done.

Accounts receivable is part of the many accounting transactions that take place within a business setting. The concept revolves around billing clients who owe a either an individual or organization for goods or services they received. This procedure is done by creating an invoice, mailing and finally, sending it out to every client who owes a business money.

Accounts receivable is an important practice in any organization because it used to measure a firm's effectiveness when it comes to extending credit facilities to its customers as well as implementing proper and efficient debt collection techniques. It's important to mention that the receivables turnover ratio is an activity ratio that gauges how a firm utilizes its assets. The most commonly used formula is that the accounts receivable turnover is equal to the net credit sales divided by the average accounts receivable.

Net sales refer to the amount that a business gets from a buyer after the costs associated with the sale have been subtracted. This amount is computed by the following formula;

Gross sales - freight allowed/cash discounts/allowance for damaged or missing goods/merchandize for returned credit. On the other hand, Average receivables refer to a firm's accounts receivables (money supposed to be paid to a business) minus bad debts. For instance, if a company fails to be paid for 5% of its sales, the net receivables becomes 95% (100% - 5%) of the accounts receivable.

There are some reports from companies which only reflect the values for sales and this can have an impact on the ratio based on the amount of cash sales. By practicing accounts receivable, a company gives its clients an opportunity to benefit from interest-free loans. A high ratio means that a firm either does its business on a cash basis or it has an efficient mechanism of extending credit facilities and good collection of accounts receivable. A low ratio implies that a company needs to reevaluate its credit policies in order to ensure that debts clients owe the business are collected in a more timely and efficient manner without straining client relations.

Before implementing accounts receivable, it is important for companies to do good research and think of the best way to give credit to clients without necessarily hurting business operations.

What is Inventory?

Inventory is a common term that a lot of us have heard about. Inventory is a collection of goods, merchandize or stock. These items are known to have a value and you can either buy them from another individual or company or manufacture them by yourself and sell them to clients at a higher price compared to what you spent on purchasing them or manufacturing them. Inventory is categorized as current assets because companies always have an intention of selling them within a year from the date they are indicated on the balance sheet.

In order to understand inventories better, the following are some examples of businesses that deal with inventory.

Example 1: Company A sells both Nike and Adidas shoes. These products qualify to be classified as inventory because this company purchases them the manufacturer and sells them to its clients at higher selling prices with the aim of making profits.

Example 2: Company B sells cars. The first question that many would want to ask is "are cars really inventory?" Well, motor vehicles ideally belong to the category of fixed assets in the balance sheet. However, in this example, the business keeps cars in stock with an intention of selling them as part of business activities. In this case, the sale of the cars is targeted to be completed within a year. Because they are the main product Company B is dealing with, these cars are classified as inventory under current assets in the balance sheet.

Example 3: Company C is a property investment firm that specializes in selling both land and buildings. In as much as land and buildings are considered to be fixed assets in the balance sheet, they are inventory or current assets because this company is only keeping them for the purpose of selling them to clients as part of its business mandate. Since these sales are intended to be executed within a year, they quality to be classified as inventory.

From the above examples, it is clear that inventory doesn't mean small items that are disposed of quickly. Classifying an item as an inventory doesn't depend on the size of an asset or how fast one can secure a buyer for it. The main factor that qualifies an asset as an inventory is what the intentions a business has for the asset. If the asset has been manufactured or has been purchased elsewhere with the purpose of reselling it at a profit, it is correct to refer to the asset as inventory.

Most of you might be wondering what becomes of businesses that offer services and not products in relation to the definition of an inventory. Services businesses primarily deal with the provision of a service and include banking, hospitals, and electrical services, tailoring and accounting services among others. Businesses dealing with manufacturing and trading can be best described as those whose trading mechanism revolves around inventory sales. However, before going deeper, it is good to thoroughly understand what manufacturing and trading businesses are and their relationship with inventory.

Trading businesses are those that purchase inventory at a reduced price with the aim of reselling assets to sellers at a higher price in order to realize a profit. Examples of trading businesses include supermarkets, clothing stores, shoes stores, hardware stores among others. These businesses rely on wholesalers or manufacturers to supply them with merchandize for the purposes of reselling at retailer prices.

On the other hand, manufacturing businesses don't buy products but instead, design and make their own products using various raw materials. Once the manufacturing process has been successfully completed, the products are then sold to consumers at a price that will generate a profit. Some examples of manufacturing businesses are bakeries, car manufacturers and construction companies.

Interestingly, there is also another category of businesses that deals heavily with inventory and consists of companies that gather and extract natural resources and sell them to consumers in a more refined form. Companies in this category include farmers and mining firms. For instance, firms that deal with gold don't manufacture it, they simply extract it and sell it to consumers. The same case applies to farmers who grow and nurture their crops which they then sell to consumers with the hope of making profits.

Because of their nature of business, it has challenging to categorize farmers and miners as either trading or manufacturing business. However, the whole idea behind the above explanations and examples is to facilitate a clearer understanding of what inventory is and how it applies to various business scenarios.

What are Liabilities?

Liabilities and assets are common terms that are discussed in the realm of business. Before engaging in any form of business, it is important to know what liabilities are and how they affect your business operations and financial documents. Liabilities simply refer to a company's obligations that is a list of transactions indicating the goods and services a company has received from its creditors and required to be paid for. Liabilities often refer to past credit transactions and have the word 'payable' included in the account title. Aside from the owner's equity, liabilities can also be viewed as a company's source for assets. On the other hand, they can also be taken as a claim against a firm's assets. For instance, if a firm's balance sheet indicates total assets of $ 120,000 which is $80,000 in owner's equity and $ 40,000 in Accounts Payable. This means that creditors have the right to lay claim on company's assets. Likewise, the owner can lay claim to the remaining portion after Accounts Payable have been settled.

Liabilities also include money that has been received in advance to cater for future services. Because the amount that has been received and recorded as cash has not yet been earned, the company has to desist from reporting this as revenue and instead, indicate it as a liability. Examples here include customer deposits or unearned revenues. It's worth mentioning that there are different types of liability accounts that are often include on the balance sheet. Some of them include;

Notes payable: This is the amount that is due on the principal on a formal written commitment to pay for goods or services delivered.

Accounts Payable: This account gives a detailed account of the funds a company owes others for the goods and services that have been delivered but have not been paid for. It's worth mentioning that this account is also known as trade payables.

Salary Payable: This is a current liability account that indicates the amount of salaries that are due for payment to employees but have not been released yet.

Wages Payable: This account is indicated as a current liability and shows that amounts that are supposed to be paid to employees who worked overtime but have not yet received their dues as the time the balance sheet was being prepared.

Interest Payable: This account shows details of interest a company owes in reference to the balance sheet date.

Remember that future interest is not considered to be a liability.

Other Accrued Expenses Payable: This account gives details of obligations that a company has incurred but they are yet to be recorded in the Accounts Payable account.

Income Taxes Payable: This account reflects how much income taxes are supposed to paid to the local, state and federal governments.

Customer Deposits: This account shows how much cash has been paid in advance in order to facilitate the sending of goods and services to a customer. The corresponding entries on a company's books at the time the payments are made is entered as a debit to case and a Customer Deposits credit entry.

Warranty Liability:

This is a liability account that gives detailed of the how much a company needs to spend in order to either repair or replace a product that has been returned by a customer within its warranty period. Liability amount is often specified and recorded when the sale is taking place and it is the same time the expense is reported. A Warranty Payable is also referred to as a Warranty Liability and is classified as a contingent liability.

Lawsuit Payable, Unearned Revenues and Bond Payables among other accounts are some of the common liabilities account we often see in the balance sheet. It is also worth mentioning that liability accounts are normally associated with credit balances.

What are contra liabilities? These are liability accounts that have debit balances. This is an account that is a contra of the traditional credit balance associated with a liability account. Examples of contra liability accounts are Discount on Bonds Payable and Discount on Notes Payable. Understanding the different types of liabilities account is critical to ensure accurate reporting as well as be fully aware of the liabilities associated with a business.

Types of Liabilities

Liabilities are a common term that is used in accounting to imply amounts that a business owes to other parties. A balance sheet is a critical for the survival of any business because it helps to determine the Net Worth of a business and company liabilities are a key determinant of determining the net worthiness of a company. In order to understand how to deal with liabilities in a business and how to record them in various financial documents, it is important to know that there are different types of liabilities and they fall into two main categories which are fixed and current liabilities.

However, it is important to mention that aside from these two categories, other types of liabilities also exist.

Fixed liability: These are liabilities that are often paid when a company has dissolved and is winding up. Examples of fixed liability are Surplus, Capital and Reserve. As an entrepreneur, it is important to evaluate your business and understand what your fixed liabilities are. By doing this, it becomes to easier to monitor and account for them in various financial documents such as balance sheets.

Long-term liability: Liabilities that a company has not planned to offset within the next accounting period are referred to as long-term liabilities. From the name, these are liabilities take a long time to repay and examples include Mortgage, Large loans to undertake major corporate projects and Debentures of a company among others. A lot of businesses in operation have long term liabilities which are critical for the success of a business. Identifying your long term liabilities and knowing how they should be accurately recorded in financial documents is essential.

Current liability: This is an expense which needs to be offset within the next financial trading period. Unlike long-term liabilities which take long to be paid, current liabilities on the other hand are short term expenses and they include Bank overdraft, Bills Payable, Sundry, creditors among others.

Trade liability: Sundry period and Bill Payable are examples of trade liabilities. This is a liability which comes about as a result of services and goods which have been supplied to clients.

Financial liability: This is a liability that a business incurs as a result of financial transactions or purposes. An example is a bank overdraft or a short term loan.

Contingent liability: This is not a liability that has actually taken place already but is expected to become a reality in the event that the unexpected happens. This liability is more of a provision set aside to cater for unforeseen events that may happen in the future. Examples of contingent liability include liability for pending court cases just in case a company loses a lawsuit and is required to incur some expenses. Another example is Bills discounted before maturity.

Wise entrepreneurs always have a good understanding of the different types of liabilities incurred by their businesses. It is always good to have set up mechanisms in place that ensure the various types of liabilities are accurately recorded in various financial documents to reflect an accurate financial picture of the business. At the end of the day, it is all about how transparent you are in your dealings.

What is a Technical Analysis?

A lot of you must have heard of the term technical analysis especially if you are into stock trading. So, what exactly does technical analysis mean? This is a topic that many investors would like to shy away from because they find it boring. However, technical analysis is an important concept if you want to break through in day trading. The only way to succeed as a day trader is to have access to plenty of accurate information in order to make quick and accurate decisions. There are a lot of things you need to know about the market, stock market practices as well as trends. In order to comfortably achieve all this, technical analysis unlocks a lot of knowledge and opportunities that you can use to your advantage.

Technical analysis is the study of market figures and facts. Individuals who practice technical analysis principles are likely to obtain better returns than traders who ordinarily trade on the market. Technical analysis is important because technical analysts design programs, charts, rules and graphs in reference to the figures and formulas that exist within the market. Technical analysis is critical for any investor because it helps one to predict future market trends. Using technical analysis, it is possible for investors to make arrangement based on accurate information to know which stocks to purchase and which ones should be sold.

An analysis usually facilitates firms to make investments with using both their money as well as their clients' money. It's worth mentioning that investment firms also earn their revenue by helping investors to find suitable investments for their money. Technical analysis comes with a lot of pressure to be on top of things but the rewards are definitely exciting.

So, how is technical analysis for a typical trader? You shouldn't worry if you lack adequate mathematical skills to understand technical analysis. However, you are free to utilize their studies for your benefit. Technical analysts are well respected in the industry because a lot of people listen to their observations. Since they are professionals, they always have an in-depth view of the market. If you're keen on becoming a successful day trader, you should pay close attention to the observations and recommendations of stock market technical analysts.

Besides technical analysis, there are several other ways to gain access to credible market information. Attending a market trading school is highly beneficial because not only do you learn useful market skills from technical analysts, you also get a chance to learn directly from experienced traders who have succeeded in the financial markets. You need to ensure that you select a reputable school that is reputable that organizes seminars that will keep you updated with market trends.

The internet is a wealth of information that is highly beneficial if you need to move in the right direction. Thankfully, various internet platforms have broken down the concept of technical analysis making it easier for traders and investors who don't have a finance and investment background to understand what this theory is all about. Facilities such as online trading chat rooms can complement your efforts of using technical analysis and give you vital information of different market trends. With this information, you can have a good idea of what is happening in the market.

The advantage of technical analysis programs is that they permit you to sample market systems and practice trading using fake money. Doing this is a great way to have an understanding of how markets perform. So, in summary, technical analysis is simply a set of graphs and charts that enable industry players to have an accurate picture of what is happening in the market. When you are aware of what is happening on the market, it gives you a better chance to excel and reap good returns. Technical analysis is an important topic for anyone who is willing to be a stock trading guru.

What is a Fundamental Analysis?

Unlike technical analysis, fundamental analysis dwells on the analysis and financial statement of a business and general company health. Fundamental analysis focuses more on an in-depth analysis of a company on issues such as market competition, management and the current trading environment. Furthermore, fundamental analysis is keen on evaluating the competitive advantage of a company when compared to other industry players.

The role of fundamental analysis cannot be underestimated when it comes to where to invest funds. Furthermore, this analysis seeks to find out more about a company's performance both in the present as well as in the past. This analysis is deep rooted and leaves nothing to chance when it comes to digging for information and looking for the truth. Aside from assessing the viability of markets, fundamental analysis is also used to screen forex market economies as well as gauge the overall performance of the economy.

Fundamental analysis makes use of two approaches which are the top down analysis and the bottom up analysis. While technical analysis makes use of present data and uses it to predict future happenings through prices, trends, volumes and charts , fundamental analysis on the other hand takes into account both the current and past data for purposes of forecasting. Fundamental analysis aims to assist in analyzing business performance, risk calculation, evaluating business decisions and stock evaluation.

Based on the above explanations, it is safe to say that fundamental analysis plays a major role in the analysis of stocks. Before beginning to trade, it is good to carry out a market analysis in order to increase your chances of winning in your trade and getting good profits.

Fundamental explication basically revolves around examining a country's economy in order to predict the currency status of a nation. There are several factors that influence a country's economy i.e. inflation, Gross Domestic Product among others. These factors are critical for the development of an economy and also have an impact on the country's currency.

If you choose to use fundamental analysis in your trading, you need to keep track on how an economy is performing. You don't need to worry as this is something simple you can do on your own by checking what is currently happening in the country and what effects it has on the currency levels.

It's important to note that there are news that have a large scale effect on a country's economic performance and you need to keep this in mind when doing fundamental analysis. Trade balances, CPI (Consumer Profit Index), Retail Sale, FOMC (Federal Open Market Committee Reports) among others are some of the key events. Aside from these, the overall economic performance of a country is affected by factors such as War, Natural disasters, Local elections and war. In such cases, there are always major changes that are experienced in the currency value.

Aside from having the intention to invest, fundamental analysis is an eye opener of how a company is performing financially. There is a need to come up with strategies to help a firm especially if it is undergoing turbulent times financially. For anyone who is planning to invest and looking for information, having a comprehensive report on fundamental analysis and going through it before making a decision is the best approach to take before putting money into any investment venture.

A good number of auditing procedures revolve around fundamental analysis, qualitative and technical technique. After performing all these procedures, it is up to an investor to make a decision and determine whether the market they wish to enter is too risky for them or it is a safe investment with a promise of good returns.

Why Should the Balance Sheet Important to You?

There are two primary tools that can enable you to effectively manage your finances. The budget and the balance sheet are the most favorite and financial consultants believe they are the key to achieving financial independence. The only way to understand and succeed in personal financing is to have a good understanding of both the balance sheet and budget. If you learn how to use them well, you have a full snapshot of your finances.

A balance sheet is very important because it shows you how and where to tap opportunities. It is essential because it shows you the need to have a clear personal financial picture. The main highlights in a balance sheet is not the assets but is your net worth because this is what you currently hold and can call yours. The sum total of your liabilities subtracted from assets gives you the Net Worth. After you have done all your calculations on your balance sheet, the ultimate value is the Net Worth. You can have a positive, negative or zero net worth. Below are some of the scenarios that lead to these results.

Negative Net Worth: If your net worth is in the negative range, it means you are doing badly when it comes to managing your finances. Your balance sheet is your report card and such as result means that you have failed. However, this shouldn't worry so much because there are appropriate measures that you can take to rectify this situation. If you are planning and managing your finances with the goal of saving and living a comfortable retirement life, your net worth should be on an upward trend.

Positive Net Worth: With a positive net worth, you can comfortably deal with any financial emergencies and come out victorious. When time comes for you to retire, your net worth should be far on the positive side in order for you to lower your costs and have enough money to invest. Remember that at this time, you need to replace your past income with a sound investment venture that can give you steady earnings. Growing your net worth requires years of nurturing, dedication and commitment.

Zero or Near Zero Net Worth: There are instances when it is okay to have a net worth of zero or near zero especially when you are just beginning the journey to achieve financial prosperity. At this time, you may have just started working and are required to pay student loans with the hope that your job will enable you to secure higher finances in future. It is important to mention that this is your best time to start working on building your net worth. Beginning this process early in life is the wisest thing to do as it will save you the stress of having to work too hard later in future. However, it's sad to note that a lot of people find themselves in their 30's and 40's without a net worth. In this case, you will be forced to work hard in order to prepare for financial challenges that you will face. The good thing is that you could have made some mistakes in the past which you can use to learn. Financial undisciplined youth always pay for the consequences much later in life because of not utilizing balance sheets and other critical personal financial documents.

When you balance sheet indicates a positive net worth, you know you are accumulating your assets and also controlling your debt which is a good step. The key of a positive balance sheet is that your debts offset the value of your assets and eventually, your debt/equity ratio should be below one and becoming lesser as time goes by.

Having a balance sheet is the only way you can keep track and know what is happening with your finances. Thanks to the balance sheet, a lot of individuals have realized their mistakes earlier and become wiser when it comes to managing personal finances. in order to succeed, you must pay keen attention on your balance sheet in order to pinpoint opportunities for financial growth. Your financial power and capability lies in your net worth and its only the balance sheet that guarantees you this freedom.

Understanding the Balance Sheet

When you plan to begin a business or invest in one, there are several financial terms and documents that you need to understand. It is always advisable to seek the help of a qualified professional in order to have a good idea of what you are doing as well as be able to correctly interpret financial documents. As much as it is understood that you cannot know everything, there are simple concepts that you need to understand regardless of your financial background. A balance sheet is an important financial document for every business that is in operation.

So, what is a balance sheet? This document is a reflection of a firm's financial standing and also measures the net worth at a specified period of time. Unlike other financial documents which measure performance over a period of time, a balance sheet is fixed and indicates the value of a business at a given specific time period.

What is contained in a balance sheet? This document shows the total assets that a business owns as well as the sum of its liabilities. In this case, liabilities refer to the debts that a business owes other parties. They include loans, mortgages and other borrowed materials. The other information contained in a balance sheet is the particulars of the owner's equity as well as funds contributed by shareholders. Any profits that a business has managed to retain over the years are also included in the balance sheet. Shareholder's equity is also referred to a company's net worth and is the total sum of assets minus a company's liabilities.

So, what is the purpose of a balance sheet? The balance sheet is a summary of the financial position of a company. The balance sheet is a comprehensive document that not only gives a list of the items owned or controlled by a company but also indicates what the company owes others.

A good balance sheet should be accurate and well prepared. It should also clearly reflect the value of a company's total assets, the sum value of shareholders equity as well as the liabilities of a company. It is important to mention that in order to understand what the balance sheet is and the role in plays, there are 5 basic things about it that you need to understand. These are; current assets, fixed assets, equity, current liabilities and long term liabilities.

The term current is used in this context to refer to a period of one year or less from the date of the balance sheet preparation. Therefore, in the same context, current assets refer to the hard cash that was available in the company during the one year or assets that were converted into cash during the period. It's important to mention the current assets include the inventory as well as the accounts receivable. Companies that offer services don't have an inventory and therefore, only a total amount of cash and accounts receivable are put into consideration.

Fixed assets refer to the equipment a company has invested in that have an effect on the accounting processes. Typically, machinery, vehicles, buildings and other items used on a daily basis are categorized as fixed assets. A net fixed asset is the difference between the actual amounts spent on purchase subtract the depreciated value.

Current liabilities refer to debts that will be settled within the year from the date the balance sheet is prepared while long term liabilities are long term debts such as mortgages and other long term debts.

Equity is a general term referring to equity from shareholders, treasury stock, preferred stocks, paid-up capital and retained capital.

With the above descriptions of what a balance sheet entails, it should be simple for an individual to go through and understand the details of a balance sheet. However, the most critical aspect is to know how to interpret the balance sheet in order to make the appropriate investment and other financially related decisions. Publicly traded companies are required by law to release their financial statements to the public which includes balance sheets. This means that if you are planning to invest, it is important to know what financial statements are relevant and how you plan to use the information you have obtained for your benefit.

Book Review

Thank you for reading my book Basic Understanding of Bond Investments Book Five - for Teens and Young Adults. Please, if you liked the book take a spare moment as it would be a great help if you could post a review of it on Amazon and let other potential readers know why you liked it. It's not necessary to write a lengthy, formal review—a summary of the comments from you would be perfectly fine.

About the Author

Ronald E. Hudkins (1951-Present) now residing in Durango, Colorado was born in Canton, Ohio and raised in Massillon, Ohio. He was drafted into military service in 1970 where he remained up until 1993 when he retired honorably from the U.S. Army, Military Police Corps. During his service, after and in between a lot of traveling he attended many universities that include Kent State

University, Maryland University, Central Texas College (European Branch), Blair Junior College, Hagerstown Junior College and Phoenix University. He declared two majors in the areas of Business Administration and a Bachelor of Science in Information Technology.

The Author
Ronald E. Hudkins

Ronald has been writing as a hobby for over twenty years. He has completed a collection of multiple genres in both fiction and nonfiction that include financial, estate, cooking and identity theft. In the area of fiction he has published humor, science fiction and fantasy. He is polishing up some children's, paranormal romance, romance and additional science fiction books. He has approximately 50 additional plot outlines completed and their associated books in various stages of completion. We can anticipate more stories in the areas of finance, children's and young adult reading as well as humor, fantasy, romance, thrillers and even some mystery and steampunk. Only the author's files and mind know the definitive creations yet to be.

He is a Platinum Level Expert author at http://ezinearticles.com/expert=Ronald_Hudkins where he has published over 100 articles in 29 separate niches which have amassed over 74,000 views.

He participates on social sites, such as Facebook and Twitter, videos on YouTube and slid presentations too many and numerous to list. Needless to say, he stays occupied and busy and as such - we all benefit. See his other projects page on his author website at: http://www.ronaldhudkins.com

Authors Other Books Fiction

Book 3 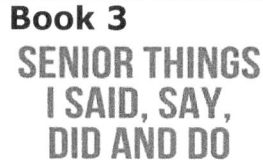 **Dec 21, 2013**	**Book 4** 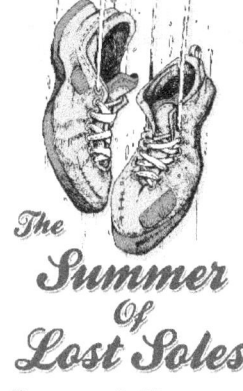 **Mar 20, 2013**
Book 5  **Nov 16 2013**	**Book 7**  **Pending Apr 2015**
Book16  **Aug 28, 2014**	**Book 17**  **Sep 16, 2014**

Book 9  Mar 19, 2014	

Authors Other Books Nonfiction

Book 6  Dec 26, 2013	Book 13 Aug 12, 2014
Book 12	Book 8

Aug 22, 2014

Book 19

Mar 7, 2014

Book 20

Feb 4, 2015

Book 11

Feb 8 2015

Book 18

June 12, 2014

Book 14

100 Easy Holiday Platter
Appetizers for New Years

Jan 20, 2015

Book 1

Oct 27, 2014

Jul 12, 2007

Book 2

Jun 15, 2011

Just for Fun

Humor Magazine

Authors Adult Books Romance/Erotica

Book 10	Book 15
May 10, 2014	Aug 24, 2014

See author's wholesale and retail outlets at the following site;

The Author's Books are generally available in the following formats;

V	Medium Options	V
Android	Desktop	Tablet
eReader	Windows	IOS
	Smartphone	
Audio	Paperback	ePub
^	Format Options	^

Thank You for the Visit !!!

Investing for Profit

If you are looking for some of the very best investment programs and services relative to Commodities, Forex, Options, Personal Finance, Real Estate and Stocks this page has you covered. Remember, the right knowledge can mean the difference between significant gains and catastrophic losses. We're here to give you the right knowledge for each market. http://www.ronaldhudkins.com/investments.html

About Investing for Profit

If you are guessing or simply do not know what you are doing in the world of investment you can lose a lot of your hard earned money. Sure, you can get lucky and actually establish some profitable investments but you can also see your profits get wiped out in an instant. However with the proper guidance, tools and self-help education you can learn to limit any losses in any market and these reference books are designed specifically to show you how.

When you visit my Investing for Profit digital library you will find the absolute top of the line investment programs and services that are currently or about to be available. It does not matter where your interests are held be it in Stocks, FOREX, options, real estate or stocks this site will keep you investing intelligently. You know as well as I the difference between exceptional gains or disastrous losses boils down to just having the correct knowledge. At this site you have the complete and correct knowledge no matter which market you invest in.

One of the best things about the Investing for Profit Mall is the selection of programs that are available. Different sectors and trading styles can be hot at various times. When there is a bull market in natural gas, gold or oil you can check out the many featured programs in the commodities trading area. If the stock market is sinking maybe other investment option programs are right for you. This site allows you to educate yourself completely for whatever market you choose to place your investments.

Appendix I - Glossary of Terms

A

Accrual-type Savings Security

A savings bond or note that increases in value periodically as interest is added to the security's issue price.

Accrued Interest

The amount of interest a security earns before it is issued. In most cases, securities don't earn interest before they're issued. They do when the security is sold in a reopening or when the security's dated date falls on a weekend or holiday. In these two circumstances, an investor may have to pay accrued interest when he or she buys a security. However, if an investor pays accrued interest, he or she gets the money back in the next interest payment. (The payment to the investor covers a full six-month interest-earning period. The investor's payment to the government covers a shorter time frame at the start of that six-month period.) In this arrangement, the net interest paid to the investor is the interest earned only after the security is issued to him or her.

Accrual-Basis Tax Reporting

Reporting the interest earned each year for a security.

Administered Estate

An estate being administered or otherwise settled by a court.

Administrator

A person appointed by a court to administer (or otherwise settle) the estate of a deceased person.

Announcement Date

The date the U.S. Treasury notifies the public of an upcoming auction. The auction announcement states the securities to be auctioned, date of the auction, dollar amount to be offered, and more.

Appreciation-type Savings Security

A security for which the interest earned is reported each year. See Accrual-type Savings Security.

Auction

An auction is how the U.S. Treasury sells Treasury bills, Treasury notes, Treasury bonds, and Treasury Inflation-Protected Securities (TIPS). Competitive bids submitted in an auction determine a security's interest rate or discount rate, and price. However, investors who buy securities through TreasuryDirect or Legacy Treasury Direct don't bid competitively—that is, they don't specify the rate they will accept. Rather, they agree to accept whatever terms are established by the competitive bids.

Auction Announcement

A press release that states the security to be auctioned, date of the auction, dollar amount to be offered and other information.

Auction Date

The date when the U.S. Treasury sells a Treasury bill, Treasury note, Treasury bond, or Treasury Inflation-Protected Security (TIPS). Tentative auction dates are released months in advance. A date becomes official when the auction is formally announced; usually, a few days before the auction.

Automated Clearing House (ACH)

A secure system to transfer funds that acts as the central clearing facility for Electronic Fund Transfer (EFT) transactions.

B

Baby Bonds

A name originally given to the Series A-1935 savings bond, but carried over to Series B-1936, C-1937 & 1938, and D-1939, 1940, & 1941 (through April) savings bonds.

Backup Withholding

Backup withholding is the amount of money withheld by the Fiscal Service to satisfy debts owed by the taxpayer to the IRS.

Bank

A depository financial institution such as a bank or credit union.

Bank Account Type

The type of bank account (e.g., checking or savings) used when a payment or debit is processed in TreasuryDirect.

Beneficiary

The individual designated on the bond who becomes the owner of the bond upon the death of the bond's owner. Bonds bearing the name of a beneficiary are registered, for example, "John Smith Payable on Death (POD) to Jane Smith." "Jane Smith" is the beneficiary.

Beneficiary Under a Trust

The person for whom a trust is created or who is entitled to the income from a trust.

Bequest

A bequest is a gift, given to the recipient upon the death of the donor. Bequests are typically designated in wills.

Bill

See Treasury Bill.

Bond

See Treasury Bond or Savings Bond.

Bond Call

See Called Bond.

Bond of Indemnity

A bond of indemnity is a document that obligates one or more parties to perform a certain act or pay a penalty. The bond of indemnity states the specific amount of the penalty.

Book-Entry

Securities maintained as electronic records rather than in paper form.

Budget surplus

When an individual or organization has more money than is necessary to cover its expenses.

Bureau of Public Debt

The Bureau of the Public Debt (BPD) was an agency in the U. S. Department of the Treasury which managed the borrowing of money needed to run the federal government and accounts for the national debt. The Bureau of the Public Debt consolidated with the Financial Management Service in October 2012 into the Bureau of the Fiscal Service.

C

Called Bonds

A Treasury bond the U.S. Treasury redeems before the bond's maturity date. Only Treasury bonds issued before 1985 are subject to being called. When a bond is called, the U.S. Treasury states the date when the bond will stop paying interest.

Cash-Basis Tax Reporting

Reporting all of the interest earned over the life of the security in the year that it reaches final maturity, is redeemed, or otherwise disposed.

Cash Management Bill

A Treasury bill not offered according to a schedule, but offered as the government's borrowing needs warrant. Terms vary widely, from a few days to hundreds of days. Cash management bills aren't sold in TreasuryDirect. However, cash management bills originally offered as 26- or 52-week bills can be transferred into TreasuryDirect.

Certificate of Indebtedness (C of I)

See Zero-Percent Certificate of Indebtedness.

Certification

Process by which a bank or other financial institution guarantees a signature in the request for payment on a savings bond, reissue, or other request relating to savings bonds.

Certified Copy

The copy of original legal documents that contain a raised or impressed seal plus statements about the accuracy and authenticity of the document.

Certifying Officer

An officer or other employee of a bank, trust company, or credit union, who is expressly authorized by the institution to certify or guarantee signatures.

Closed Book Period

Before the payment date for a specific marketable security, the period in which an investor cannot conduct transactions for that security. In TreasuryDirect, the period is four business days. In Legacy Treasury Direct, the period is 10 business days.

Commercial Book-Entry System

The system in which banks, brokers, and dealers hold Treasury bills, Treasury notes, Treasury bonds, and Treasury Inflation-Protected Securities (TIPS) on behalf of investors. For the investor, the alternative to this system is to hold securities directly with the government through either TreasuryDirect or Legacy Treasury Direct.

Competitive Bidding

A type of bidding where the investor specifies the discount rate or yield he or she will accept for a security that will be auctioned. This type of bidding is available only in the Commercial Book-Entry System. Investors who use TreasuryDirect or Legacy Treasury Direct engage in noncompetitive bidding; this means they agree to accept any discount rate or yield determined by the auction.

Convert

A method to change your paper savings bonds to electronic securities.

Consumer Price Index (CPI)

The consumer price index (CPI) measures changes through time in the price level of consumer goods and services purchased by households. In the United States, the CPI is defined by the United States Bureau of Labor Statistics as "a measure of the average change over time in the prices paid by urban consumers for a market basket of consumer goods and services." The CPI-U, or the Consumer Price Index for all Urban Consumers is used to adjust the principal of a Treasury Inflation-Protected Security (TIPS) and to determine the inflation rate component of the I Bond interest rate.

Co-Owner

The person named second in the registration of a Treasury security whose name is preceded by the word "OR." Both co-owners have equal rights to the security. For example, "John Smith OR Jane Smith." "Jane Smith" is the co-owner.

Coupon (or Coupon Rate)

The interest rate stated on a bond when it is issued. The coupon is typically paid twice a year.

Current Income Savings Bond

A H or HH savings bond, on which interest is paid every six months, usually via Direct Deposit, to the owner or co-owners. H and HH bonds are no longer available for purchase.

Current Value

The amount of money a security is worth at a specific point in time.

Current Redemption Value (CRV)

What a bond is worth at a specific point in time, if the holder were to cash it in.

CUSIP (Committee for Uniform Security Identification Procedures)

CUSIP is the unique number Treasury uses to identify securities maturing on a specific date.

Custom Account

This is a flexible account within a TreasuryDirect account that you may establish to meet your specific financial goals.

D

Dated Date

The date when a Treasury note, Treasury bond, or Treasury Inflation-Protected Security (TIPS) begins earning interest. The dated date and issue date are usually the same. The dates are different when a security is sold in a reopening or when the dated date falls on a weekend or holiday. In both of those cases, the dated date comes before the issue date.

Debt Ceiling

The maximum amount the U.S. government is allowed to be in debt. The figure is set by Congress. As the government nears the limit, Treasury may suspend its sales of securities, as selling securities would put the government further into debt.

Decedent

A person who has died.

Definitive Security

A security in paper form.

De-Linking

De-linking refers to moving the linked account's securities to a primary TreasuryDirect account. The only linked account that TreasuryDirect customers can de-link is a minor account.

Delivery

The moving of a gift security from the TreasuryDirect account of the purchaser to the TreasuryDirect account of the recipient.

You must hold savings bonds in your TreasuryDirect account for at least five business days before you can deliver them to the gift recipient. The five-day hold protects Treasury against loss by ensuring the ACH debit has been successfully completed before the funds can be moved.

Denomination

The dollar amount shown on the face of the security (also referred to as "face amount" or "face value").

Direct Deposit

The automatic deposit of payments to a checking or savings account at a financial institution. Direct deposit of interest payments on Series HH/H bonds is required on all bonds purchased October 1989 and later. HH/H bonds with issue dates prior to that date may be directly deposited.

Discount

The difference between the par amount and price of a marketable security, when the price is less than the par amount. Discount is referred to as "refund" on the Legacy Treasury Direct *Statement of Account*. A discount is the opposite of a premium.

Discount Rate

The rate of return, on an annual basis, on Treasury bills held until they mature. The discount rate is expressed in percentage terms and based on a 360-day year.

Dispositions

To transfer management or care of a TreasuryDirect account to another person or entity, such as with a Power of Attorney.

E

Earnings Rate

A combination of two rates: a fixed rate of return and a semiannual inflation rate. (Series I Bonds only)

E Bond

A savings bond previously offered by the U.S. Department of the Treasury. An E Bond is an accrual-type security, with interest added to the bond on the first day of each six-month accrual cycle and paid upon redemption.

EE Bond

A United States Savings Bond offered by the U.S. Department of the Treasury, an EE Bond is an accrual-type security, meaning interest is added to the bond monthly or every six months (depending upon the original issue date) and paid upon redemption.

Education Feature

Interest earned on EE bonds with January 1, 1990, and later issue dates may qualify for exclusion from income for Federal income tax purposes if the owner pays his or her tuition and required fees or those of his or her spouse or legally dependent children at colleges, universities, and qualified technical schools during the year eligible bonds are redeemed. Costs of room, board, and books are excluded.

See IRS Publication 550 "Investment Income and Expenses and IRS Form 8815 for details.

Electronic Deposit

A credit transaction initiated through electronic means (i.e., phone, computer network) by a financial institution or payroll office.

EFT (Electronic Funds Transfer)

The automatic deposit of payments to a checking or savings account at a financial institution. Direct deposit of interest payments on Series HH/H bonds is required on all bonds purchased October 1989 and later. HH/H bonds with issue dates prior to that date may be directly deposited.

Employee Retirement Income Security Act of 1974 (ERISA)

ERISA is the U. S. federal law that sets minimum standards for pension plans in private industry. It also has many rules on the federal income tax effects of transactions associated with employee benefit plans. ERISA was enacted to protect the interests of employee benefit plan participants and their beneficiaries. ERISA

- requires that plans disclose financial and other information about the plan;
- sets standards of conduct for plan fiduciaries; and
- provides for appropriate remedies and access to the federal courts.

Employer Identification Number (EIN, FTIN)

An Employer Identification Number (EIN) is also known as a Federal Tax Identification Number, and is used to identify a business entity.

Exchange

This term applies to the purchase of Series HH Bonds which are no longer available. "Exchange" and "Redemption-Exchange" are interchangeable terms referring to the authorized redemption (payment) of eligible securities presented and surrendered for the purpose of applying the proceeds (what they're worth) for the purchase of other securities according to Treasury regulations.

Executor

The person designated in a decedent's will to carry out the directions and requests in the will and to dispose of property according to the provisions of the will.

External Transfer

Moving the partial or full amount of a marketable security from TreasuryDirect to a bank or broker. When requesting a partial External Transfer, you must transfer a minimum of $100 while leaving at least $100 of the current value of the security. This action automatically changes the ownership of the security to the bank or broker.

Extended Maturity Period

A period of time after a savings bond reaches face value that the bond continues to earn interest. Also referred to as an extension period.

Extension Period

A period of time after a savings bond reaches face value that the bond continues to earn interest.

F

Face Amount

The dollar amount shown on the face of the security (also referred to as "face value" or "par amount").

Face Value

See Face Amount or Par Amount.

Federal Deposit Insurance Corporation (FDIC)

The Federal Deposit Insurance Corporation (FDIC) is an independent agency of the federal government. The FDIC preserves and promotes public confidence in the U.S. financial system by:

- insuring deposits in banks (keeping the money you have in the banks safe);
- managing the deposit insurance funds; and
- limiting the effect on the economy and the financial system when a bank fails.

Fiduciary

A person acting primarily for another's benefit (e.g., executor, administrator, trustee, guardian).

Fiduciary Capacity

Relates to conducting business or handling property for the benefit of another person.

Financial Institution

A financial institution is an institution (public or private) that collects funds (from the public or other institutions) and invests them in financial assets.

Final Maturity

The point at which a bond stops earning interest, also known as the final extended maturity date.

Fixed Rate

An interest rate that stays the same for the entire term of a loan or the entire life of a security.

Floating Rate Note (FRN)

A Floating Rate Note is a government security that has interest payments that rise and fall based on discount rates of 13-week Treasury bills. An FRN is issued for a term of two years and pays interest quarterly.

Freedom Shares

Bonds that Treasury issued from May of 1967 to October of 1970. Freedom shares had a final maturity of 30 years from their issue date and were originally offered in combination with Series E bonds to promote public investment in government bonds.

Also known as "savings notes".

G

Gift Bond

A gift bond is a savings bond that you buy for someone else. The owner or co-owner is the person to whom you are giving the bond. You, the buyer, are not the owner or co-owner.

Grantee

For any type of security that you own in your TreasuryDirect account, you may give other people rights to see (View) or act on (Transact) for that security. When you do that, you are the Grantor. The person whom you allow to View or Transact is the "Grantee."

Grantor

See Grantee definition above.

Guaranteed Minimum Rate

Guaranteed Minimum Rates apply to savings notes, E bonds and EE bonds issued before May 1995. A bond's Guaranteed Minimum Rate is established when the bond is issued and is subject to change at the beginning of each extended maturity period. These rates create the minimum value that a bond is worth at each interest accrual date. (On any interest accrual date, a bond may be worth more than its minimum value if its market-based rates create a higher value.)

H

H or HH Bond

See Series HH Bond

Heir

One who inherits or is entitled to inherit property

I

I Bonds

See Series I Bond

Incoming External Transfer

Moving a marketable security from a bank, broker, or Legacy Treasury Direct into an online TreasuryDirect account. For more information, see Learn more about Marketable Security Transfers.

Income Limits for Education Feature

The high end of the modified adjusted gross income of the taxpayer on which the tax benefits of the interest exclusion for the Education Savings Bond Program are based.

Individual Retirement Arrangement (IRA)

An IRA is a retirement plan that provides tax advantages for retirement savings in the United States. The term encompasses an individual retirement account — a trust or custodial account set up for the exclusive benefit of taxpayers or their beneficiaries and an individual retirement annuity, by which the taxpayers purchase an annuity contract or an endowment contract from a life insurance company.

Individual Retirement Bond

Accrual-type U.S. savings security sold to individuals eligible to participate in an Individual Retirement Arrangement (IRA). These bonds were first issued in January 1975 after enactment of the Employee Retirement Income Security Act of 1974 ("ERISA"). The sale of these bonds ended on April 30, 1982.

Inflation

Inflation is a rise in the general level of prices of goods and services in an economy over a period of time. When the general price level rises, each unit of currency buys fewer goods and services.

Inflation-Indexed Security

A security whose payment or payments are tied to inflation—specifically, to the Consumer Price Index for All Urban Consumers (CPI-U). The U.S. Treasury sells two such securities: the Series I Savings Bond and the Treasury Inflation-Protected Security (TIPS).

Inscription

Information about the owner/co-owner/beneficiaries that appears on the face of paper savings bonds. (e.g., social security account number or employer identification number, names, connectives ("OR", "POD", "Payable on death to"), and addresses.

Interest

Compensation at a specified rate, paid for the use of money.

Interest (Compound)

Interest upon interest, where accrued interest is added to the principal sum, and the whole treated as new principal, for the calculation of the interest for the next period.

Interest (Simple)

Money which is paid for the use of the principal (sum lent), at a certain rate.

Interest Accrual

Interest earned by an appreciation-type or accrual-type savings security, such as a Series EE bond, and added to what the bond was worth either at the time it was purchased or at some point thereafter according to applicable regulations.

Interest Income Statement (1099-INT)

The 1099-INT is an IRS form that lists the amount of interest a taxpayer earned on a specific investment or investments during the year. You need 1099-INTs for all of your investments to calculate your taxes and to send in with your tax form. If you have a TreasuryDirect account, you must go online after the first of each year to print the 1099-INT for your Treasury investments. If you have redeemed paper savings bonds, you will receive a 1099-INT in the mail.

Interest Rate (notes, bonds, and TIPS only)

The interest rate determines the amount of money that your money earns. Interest rate is a percentage used to figure out how much interest you will get. For example, if you have a $100 Treasury note with an interest rate of 5 percent; at the end of the year, you will get $5.00 (5% of $100) in interest.

Internal Transfer

With an internal transfer, you move part or all the value of a marketable security from one TreasuryDirect account to another. For a partial internal transfer, you must transfer at least $100 and leave at least $100 of the current value of the security. An internal transfer automatically changes the ownership of the security from one account holder to another.

Investing Maturing Proceeds

When you invest maturing proceeds, you use the money from a Bill, Note, Bond, or TIPS that is ending its paying period (that is, maturing) to buy a new security or securities. (See Learn more about Reinvesting Maturing Proceeds.)

Issue Date

For a marketable security, the issue date is the date when Treasury puts the security into the buyer's account. A security's issue date usually is the same as its dated date. For securities that Treasury sells in auctions, issue dates are published in the Tentative Auction Schedule and in auction announcements for particular auctions.

Issue Price

The issue price is the actual amount you pay to buy a savings bond.

L

Legacy Treasury Direct

Legacy Treasury Direct is the old Treasury program for holding your securities directly with the government, rather than with a bank, broker, or dealer. Established in 1986, Legacy Treasury Direct is being phased out in favor of the similar, newer program, TreasuryDirect.

Legal Representative

A legal representative is a person appointed by a court to act on behalf of the estate of someone who has died or has been declared unable to handle his or her own affairs. Legal representative is a generic term encompassing all types of representatives, including executors, administrators, personal representatives, and guardians.

Linked Accounts

TreasuryDirect Linked Accounts allow you the flexibility of managing a securities portfolio customized to your needs. You can have several accounts that are "linked" to your main account. Holdings for each Linked account are kept separately from your Primary TreasuryDirect account and from each other. Open a Minor or Custom account, or use the Conversion account to convert your paper securities into electronic form. You access your Linked accounts through your primary TreasuryDirect account.

Long-term Rate

The long-term rate applies only to interest on Series EE savings bonds with issue dates from May 1, 1995, through April 1997 and then only to interest earnings after the date these bonds are 5 years old. (See "Short-term Rate" concerning interest earned up to the date these bonds are 5 years old.)

M

Manifest

When you use SmartExchange to convert your paper bonds to electronic bonds and put them into a Treasury Direct account, you get a list of those bonds. We call that the "manifest" for your bonds. You must mail the manifest with the paper bonds that are listed on the manifest.

Market-based Interest Rate

Market-based Interest Rate is relevant only to Series E and EE savings bonds and savings notes with issue dates before May 1, 1995 that earned interest on and after November 1, 1987. The official name is "market-based variable investment yield."

Marketable Securities

Treasury bills, Treasury notes, Treasury bonds, and Treasury Inflation-Protected Securities (TIPS) are called "marketable" because owners can sell them.

Maturity

A Treasury security reaches maturity when its term expires. The security is worth its face value when it matures. However, sometimes market conditions can make the security worth its full face value before its term even expires. Also, savings bonds have an "original maturity" period during which the bond increases in value and becomes worth at least its face amount and an "extended maturity period" during which it continues to earn interest. After Treasury securities fully mature, you do not get any more extra money (interest) if you keep the securities.

Maturity Date

For marketable securities, the date when the security becomes payable and stops earning interest.

Military Safekeeping

See Safekeeping.

Minor Account

A minor is a child under the age of 18. A parent, natural guardian, or person providing chief support for a minor may set up a Minor Account and buy, hold, sell securities for the minor.

Minor

A person who is under the age of legal competence; a person under the age of majority.

N

Non-administered Estate

When someone dies, that person's estate (what the person owns) must be "settled" – distributed according to the person's will or the law. If settling the estate does not involve supervision by a court of law and no court appoints a legal representative to administer the estate that is a non-administered estate.

Noncompetitive Bid

In a U.S. Treasury auction, a noncompetitive bid is one in which an investor agrees to buy a specified number of securities at the discount rate or yield set at the auction. The limit for noncompetitive purchases is $5 million for each security type and term, for each auction. This limit applies regardless of whether buying a bill, note, bond, or TIPS and regardless of what method used to make the purchase (TreasuryDirect, broker, or dealer).

Noncompetitive Bidding

In noncompetitive bidding, the investor agrees to accept whatever discount rate or yield is determined in an auction. This is the only type of bidding offered in TreasuryDirect. The alternative to noncompetitive bidding is competitive bidding, which is available with banks, brokers, and securities dealers.

Non-Marketable Securities

Non-marketable securities can't be transferred to another owner or traded in the secondary market (examples: U.S. Savings Bonds Series EE, I, and HH).

Note

See Treasury Note.

O

Offering Amount

The total par amount of a particular security being offered in an auction.

Original Issue Date (for notes, bonds, Floating Rate Notes, and TIPS)

Date on which a specific Treasury note, Treasury bond, Floating Rate Note, or Treasury Inflation-Protected Security (TIPS) is issued for the first time. (Securities sold in reopenings are issued more than once.)

Original Issue Holding Period

TreasuryDirect requires Bills, Notes, Bonds, Floating Rate Notes, and TIPS originally issued in an account be held for 45 days before they may be internally or externally transferred. This rule doesn't apply to securities transferred into your account from an outside bank or broker.

Original Maturity

The original (or initial) term fixed for a bond. During this period, the bond increases in value and becomes worth at least its face amount.

P

Par Amount (Par Value, Face Value)

The stated value of a security on its original issue date.

Par

The principal amount of a security.

Par Value

See Par Amount.

Payroll Savings Plan

When you enroll in the Payroll Savings Plan, you buy savings bonds automatically on a regular schedule using part of what you earn. Your employer sends direct deposits to Treasury, and the bonds are issued automatically in your TreasuryDirect account once you have enough accumulated to purchase the bond you requested. See Learn More about the Payroll Savings Plan.

Penalty

If you redeem (turn in) an I bond or an EE bond in the first 5 years after the bond's issue date, you do not receive the interest for the most recent 3 months. That's a penalty.

Power of Attorney

A written and signed statement in which the person (grantor) giving the power authorizes another person (attorney-in-fact) to act on his or her behalf. The written and signed statement is called a power of attorney. The person acting under the power is called an attorney-in-fact.

Premium

The difference between the par amount and the price of a marketable security, when the price is greater than the par amount. A premium is the opposite of a discount.

Primary Account

Your primary account is your main account in TreasuryDirect. Once you have a primary account, you can set up Minor or Custom Linked accounts that you get to from your primary account.

Primary Owner

The primary owner of a security is the person who is named first in the security's registration. For example, if a security is registered as "John Doe SSN 123-45-6789 WITH Joseph Doe

SSN 987-65-4321", John Doe is the primary owner. The primary owner may grant View or Transact rights to the second-named registrant Joseph Doe.

Principal Amount

Principal amount is the same as the purchase amount of a security.

Principal Co-owner

The principal co-owner is the co-owner whose funds were used to buy the savings bonds or who received the bonds as a gift, as an inheritance, or through court proceedings and had the bonds reissued to add another person as co-owner without receiving any contribution from that other person.

Purchase Express

TreasuryDirect allows customers to quickly purchase securities using preferred registration and primary bank information or debit their bank account to fund their Zero-Percent C of I.

Purchase Limitations

The dollar amount of securities an individual can purchase in one calendar year.

Purchase Schedule

"Purchase schedule" is the phrase we use when you set up a regular schedule to buy securities in TreasuryDirect. Your purchase schedule can be monthly, quarterly, or at specific dates that you specify.

R

Rate

The amount of return on an investment in a Treasury security.

Recipient

In TreasuryDirect, this is the person who receives a gift delivery, transfer, or de-linked securities.

Redemption

The payment of what a bond or note is worth. You turn in (redeem) the bond or note and Treasury pays you its value.

Reinvesting Maturing Proceeds

Investing funds from a maturing Bill, Note, Bond, or TIPS using Zero-Percent C of I as the source of funds to purchase a new security. (See Learn more about Reinvesting Maturing Proceeds.)

Reinvestment

Reinvestment is when you buy a new security with the money you get from a matured security.

Registration

The social security number or employer identification number, names, and addresses appearing on the face of a bond. Also referred to as Inscription.

Reissue

When you want to change the names on a bond, you must ask Treasury to reissue the bond. That means you give up the bond you hold and get a new one in its place. Treasury cancels and retires the old bond and issues a new bond. The new bond has the same series, same issue date, and same total face amount as the old bond. For more on the situations which require reissuing a bond, see http://www.treasurydirect.gov/indiv/research/indepth/ebonds /res_e_bonds_eereplace.htm Reissuing a bond may have tax consequences; that is, the original owner may need to pay taxes on interest earned before the bond was reissued. See http://www.treasurydirect.gov/indiv/research/indepth/ebonds/res_e_bonds_eetaxconsider.htm for more detail.

Reopening

The auction of an additional amount of an unmatured security. A security sold at a reopening has the same maturity date and interest rate it had when originally issued. The purchase price and yield are determined at the reopening. Investors who buy a reopened security will owe accrued interest, unless the security is sold at a discount and the discount offsets the accrued interest.

Replacement

For paper savings bonds, when you report that a bond is lost, stolen, destroyed or you did not receive it, Treasury will replace it.

Reportable Event

A transaction, such as a savings bond redemption or reissue (re-registration), that requires federal income tax reporting of all interest earned from the issue date of the bond to the date of the transaction. Savings bond redemptions ordinarily are reportable events or dispositions. A reissue transaction is a reportable event if a living owner, principal co-owner, surviving co-owner, beneficiary, or other person entitled to ownership (for example, an heir upon the death of persons named on the bond) is not named owner or principal co-owner in the new registration on the bond issued in the transaction. (See IRS Publication 550, "Investment Income and Expenses.")

Request Date

The date you ask for a transaction in your TreasuryDirect account. This date may not be the date that the transaction is actually processed, based on business days, holidays, and scheduled times for transaction processing.

Retirement Plan Bonds

Retirement Plan Bonds were a type of bond that Treasury used to issue but does not issue now. From January 1975 to April 1982, they were available as an investment option for people who could make tax-deductible contributions to a "Keogh" retirement account. They were non-transferrable, accrued-interest bonds.

Return Code

An identifier resulting from the return of information by a designated financial institution. Return codes may limit the ability to conduct future transactions in TreasuryDirect.

Routing Number

The routing number is the nine-digit number associated with financial institutions (also known as ABA#). The number is usually located in the bottom left corner of a check.

S

Safekeeping

Safekeeping was a benefit offered to active duty military members who bought paper savings bonds through a payroll savings plan. This benefit allowed military members to have their bonds held by their branch of service instead of having the bonds issued and mailed directly to them.

Savings Bond

A savings bond is a security issued by the U.S. Treasury or an authorized agent showing that money has been loaned to the U.S. Government and is payable to the person to whom it is registered.

Savings Notes

Savings notes, also called "Freedom Shares," were issued from May 1967 through October 1970. They were accrual-type U.S. securities.

Savings Stamps

From at least the early 1940's until the program ended on June 30, 1970, savings stamps were acquired from post offices and sold in schools to students. Albums and patriotic materials were made available to schools to promote the program. A student could buy a $25 (face amount) Series E savings bond with as little as $18.75 in savings stamps. Stamps were non-interest bearing and unregistered.

Secondary Market

The financial market where securities that were previously issued by the Treasury are bought and sold.

Second-Named Registrant

The second person named in the registration of a security held in TreasuryDirect. In the example, "John Doe SSN 123-45-6789 WITH Joseph Doe SSN 987-65-4321," Joseph Doe is the second-named registrant.

Secure Sockets Layer (SSL)

SSL is the industry-standard protocol for keeping sensitive data, such as payment information, secure as it is being transmitted over the Internet. SSL works by using a public key to encrypt data that is transferred.

Security or Treasury Security

An obligation of debt issued by the U.S. Treasury. You lend the government money when you buy a Treasury security. Treasury securities include savings bonds, Treasury notes, Treasury bills (T-bills), Treasury bonds, and Treasury Inflation-Protected Securities (TIPS).

Series EE U.S. Savings Bond

Series EE U.S. Savings Bonds is an appreciation-type (or accrual-type) savings security issued after 1979. It is a contract between the owner or co-owners and the U. S. government. Under the contract, you, as owner or co-owner, lend money to the U. S. government, and the U.S. must repay that money with interest when the bond matures.

Series HH U.S. Savings Bond

Series HH U.S. Savings Bonds are no longer available for purchase. Because they are a 20-year non-marketable bond, some people still own HH bonds. HH bonds pay interest twice a year. The interest rate is the same (fixed) for the first 10 years after the bond's issue date. After 10 years, the interest rate is reset by the U.S. Treasury for the rest of the bond's life. Interest on HH bonds is exempt from state and local - but not federal - taxes.

Series I U.S. Savings Bonds

An inflation-indexed savings bond offered by the U.S. government. Series I bonds pay a fixed interest rate that is lower than the rate for EE savings bonds, but they also pay a variable rate that increases with inflation (as measured by the Consumer Price Index) and is recalculated semiannually. Series I bonds pay interest for up to 30 years, but there is a penalty equivalent to 3 months of earnings for redeeming the bond before 5 years.

Short-term Rate

The short-term rate applies only to interest on Series EE savings bonds with issue dates from May 1, 1995, through April 1997 and only to interest earnings up to the date these bonds are 5 years old. (See "Long-term Rate" concerning interest earned after these bonds are 5 years old.)

Signature Certification

Available at a bank or most financial institutions. Acceptable certifications include a financial institution's seal or stamp (such as Corporate Seal, Signature Guaranteed Stamp, or Medallion Stamp). Brokers must use a Medallion Stamp. Certification by a notary is ONLY acceptable for minor name corrections submitted without supporting evidence.

Social Security Number (SSN)

The identifying number issued by the Social Security Administration required on tax returns and other documents submitted to the IRS by an individual.

Single Owner

The person designated on the face of the bond as the only person entitled to redeem the bond during his or her lifetime. Also referred to as sole owner.

Sole Owner

See Single Owner.

STRIPS (Separate Trading of Registered Interest and Principal of Securities)

A fixed principal note or bond, or a Treasury Inflation-Protected Security (TIPS), whose two components, interest and repayment of principal, are separated and the principal payment becomes a separate zero-coupon security.

T

Taxpayer Identification Number

A taxpayer identification number (TIN) is either a social security number or employer identification number, depending on whether the number is assigned to an individual or to an entity, such as a trust, estate, corporation, etc. The employer identification number is assigned by the IRS.

Tax Deferral

When you defer taxes, you postpone paying them until a later date. Tax law permits you to defer taxes on the interest you earn on certain Treasury securities or in certain situations.

T-bill

See Treasury Bill.

T-bond

See Treasury Bond.

Tender

A paper form that customers of Legacy Treasury Direct can use to buy a Treasury bill, Treasury note, or Treasury Inflation-Protected Security (TIPS).

Tentative Auction Schedule

The Treasury's multi-month schedule of upcoming auctions. Though tentative, the schedule is usually accurate.

Term

For marketable securities, the length of time the security earns interest. A Treasury note, for instance, has a term of 2, 3, 5, 7, or 10 years. Marketable securities are identified by their term and type: 26-week bill, 3-year note, 20-year TIPS, for example.

TIPS (Treasury Inflation-Protected Securities)

TIPS are securities issued by the Department of Treasury whose principal increases with inflation and decrease with deflation, as measured by the Consumer Price Index.

T-note

See Treasury Note.

Trace Number

A trace number is a tracking number assigned by the Electronic Fund Transfer (EFT) process to identify individual money transfer transactions.

Transact Rights

In TreasuryDirect, for a security with Primary Owner registration, the first-named registrant (or grantor) may grant Transact rights to the second-named registrant (or grantee). The grantor may edit or delete these rights at any time. Transact rights do NOT apply to the Zero-Percent C of I security. Transact rights allow the grantee of a savings bond to view and redeem the security. Transact rights allow the grantee of a marketable security to transfer or sell the security, as well as change the maturity and/or interest payment destination. For tax reporting information, see Learn more about Tax Reporting.

Transfer

Transfer means to move the partial or full amount of a security, consisting of principal plus a proportionate amount of interest, from one TreasuryDirect account to another.

Treasury Bill (Bill, T-bill)

A Treasury bill is a government security issued in terms ranging from a few days to 52 weeks. Investors buy Treasury bills at a discount from their par amount, then receive the par amount when the bill matures. The difference between purchase price and par amount is the interest.

Treasury Bond (Bond, T-bond)

A Treasury bond is a government security issued in a term of 30 years. Investors buy Treasury bonds and then are paid interest every six months. When a Treasury bond matures, the owner is paid the bond's par amount. Treasury bonds and U.S. savings bonds are not the same.

Treasury Note (Note, T-note)

A Treasury note is a government security issued for terms ranging from 2 years to 10 years. Investors buy Treasury notes and then are paid interest every six months. When a Treasury note matures, the owner is paid the note's par amount.

Treasury Inflation-Protected Security (TIPS)

One type of government security whose payments are tied to inflation; specifically, to the Consumer Price Index for All Urban Consumers (CPI-U). Investors buy TIPS and then are paid interest every six months on the security's inflation-adjusted principal. When a TIPS matures, the owner is paid the inflation-adjusted principal or, if deflation has occurred, the original principal. TIPS are issued in terms of 5, 10, and 20 years.

Treasury Reopenings

When additional amounts of previously issued securities are issued again rather than selling new issues of those securities. The reopened securities have the same maturity date and interest rate; however, as compared to the original securities, the reopened securities have a different issue date (which creates a shorter overall term), and usually, a different purchase price.

TreasuryDirect

A web-based system for holding marketable securities and savings bonds directly with the U.S. government. For marketables, TreasuryDirect is an alternative to banks, brokers, and dealers. For savings bonds, TreasuryDirect is an alternative to paper savings bonds.

TreasuryDirect Account

Your personal online account where you can buy, transfer, redeem and otherwise manage your U.S. Treasury securities.

Trust

Property, real or personal, held by one person for the benefit of another.

Trustee

The person appointed to administer or manage a trust estate.

Trustor

The individual (in some instances, an institution or organization) who creates a trust. The Trustor may also be called the Maker, Donor, Grantor, or Settler.

U

Undelivered Payment

A payment that cannot be made to your designated financial institution and is returned to the Bureau of the Fiscal Service.

U.S. Savings Bonds

See Savings Bond.

V

Variable Rate

Any interest rate that changes on a periodic basis. Variable rates are often used for convertibles, mortgages, and certain other kinds of loans. The change is usually tied to movement of an outside indicator, such as the prime interest rate. Movement above or below certain levels is often prevented by a predetermined floor and ceiling for a given rate. Also called adjustable rate.

View Rights

In TreasuryDirect, for a security with Sole Owner registration, the first-named registrant (or grantor) may grant View rights to any individual (or grantee) with a TreasuryDirect account. On a security with Beneficiary registration, the first-named registrant may only grant View rights to the second-named registrant. On a security with Primary Owner registration, the first-named registrant may only grant View rights to the second-named registrant. The grantor may edit or delete any of these rights at any time. View rights do NOT apply to the Zero-Percent C of I security, and certain restrictions apply for converted securities.

Voluntary Guardian

A voluntary guardian is an individual who is recognized by the Department of the Treasury as authorized to act for an incapacitated person as provided in the regulations governing U.S. Savings Bonds.

W

Withholding Rate

When you will owe taxes on interest on your Treasury securities, we may withhold all or part of that amount and pay it to the IRS on your behalf. The withholding rate is the percentage of interest that we send to the IRS on behalf of the account holder. In some situations, the IRS requires a certain withholding rate. In other situations, you may voluntarily ask that we withhold a certain amount for taxes. (This is similar to withholding taxes on your pay check.)

Y

Yield

Yield is the annual rate of return on a security.

Yield from Issue Date

Yield from issue date is a percentage expressed as an annual rate that describes the overall increase in an investment's value and is a measurement of the gain from the time the investment was made or started. Such a percentage is the result of computations using the amount of the initial investment, what the investment is worth on some later date--today or in the future--and the amount of time from when the investment was made to the later date.

Z

Zero Coupons —STRIPS (Separate Trading of Registered Interest and Principal of Securities).

The principal of a stripped security and the separate interest payments are known as "zero coupons" because there are no periodic interest payments on each piece. After stripping, each piece trades separately in the secondary securities market. STRIPS can't be held in Legacy Treasury Direct or TreasuryDirect.

Zero-Percent Certificate of Indebtedness (Zero-Percent C of I or C of I)

A Treasury security that does not earn any interest. It is intended to be used as a source of funds for traditional Treasury security purchases.

Online Resources for Bond Information

GENERAL SITES

- **SEC Edgar (financial filings):** http://www.sec.gov/edgar.shtml

- **SEC Filing Alerts:** http://secfilings.com/landing.aspx?gclid=CKvk4f26nJ0CFR9N5QodVjHR7w

- **Investing in Bonds:** http://www.investinginbonds.com

- **Bonds online:** http://www.bondsonline.com

- **Barrons:** http://online.barrons.com

- **Big Charts:** http://bigcharts.marketwatch.com

- **Business Week:** http://www.businessweek.com

- **Closed-End Funds:** http://www.closed-endfunds.com/

- **CNN Money:** http://money.cnn.com

- **EFT Connect:** http://www.etfconnect.com

- **Financial Industry Regulatory Authority (FINRA):** http://www.finra.org/Investors/index.htm

- **Hoovers:** http://www.hoovers.com/free

- **Investor's Business Daily:** www.investors.com

- **Kiplinger:** https://www.kiplinger.com

- **Market Watch:** http://www.marketwatch.com

- **Mergent:** http://www.mergent.com

- **Morningstar:** http://www.morningstar.com

- **Motley Fool:** http://www.fool.com

- **NYSE Euronext (formerly American Stock Exchange):** http://www.nyse.com/home.html

- **Reuters Finance:** http://www.reuters.com/finance

- **SEC Edgar (financial filings):** http://www.sec.gov/edgar.shtml

- **SEC Filing Alerts:** http://secfilings.com/landing.aspx?gclid=CKvk4f26nJ0CFR9N5QodVjHR7w

- **Smart Money (WSJ):** http://www.smartmoney.com

- **Standard & Poor's:** http://www2.standardandpoors.com

- **The Investment Company Institute (IC) :** http://ici.org

- **Value Line:** http://valueline.com

- **Yahoo Finance:** http://finance.yahoo.com

- **Yahoo Industry Center :** http://biz.yahoo.com/ic

- **Zacks Investment Research:** http://www.zacks.com

- **Lehman Brother Aggregate Bond Index (now part of Barclays):** http://www.lehman.com/fi/indices

RATING SITES

- **Standard & Poor's:** http://www2.standardandpoors.com

- **Moody's:** http://www.moodys.com

- **Fitch:** http://www.fitchratings.com

INTERNATIONAL INFORMATION

If you are researching International funds and want information on the country go to:

- **Central Intelligence Agency World Factbook:** https://www.cia.gov/library/publications/the-world-factbook

Appendix Three

Checking Out a Brokerage Firm, Individual Broker, Investment Adviser Firm, or Individual Investment Adviser

Information about brokerage firms and individual brokers is publicly available online through FINRA's Broker Check program and by calling toll-free at (800) 289-9999. Information about certain investment adviser firms is available through the SEC's Investment Adviser Public Disclosure (IAPD) Program. Information about brokerage firms, individual brokers, ʲinvestment adviser firms and individual investment advisers also is available through each state's securities regulator. Details on how to get in touch with a state's securities regulator are available through the North American Securities Administrators Association, Inc.'s website.

FINRA's BrokerCheck Program

Information on brokerage firms. FINRA's BrokerCheck Program provides the following information on brokerage firms:

A summary report that provides an overview of the firm

A profile of the firm's ownership

A firm history, including any mergers, acquisitions or name changes

A description of the firm's operations, listing its active licenses and registrations, the types of businesses it conducts and other details

Arbitration awards and any regulatory or disciplinary events on the firm's records

Information on individual brokers. BrokerCheck provides the following information on individual brokers:

A summary report that provides an overview of the broker and his or her credentials

A listing of the broker's qualifications, including current registrations or licenses and industry exams that the broker has passed

Previous employment data for the past 10 years, both in and outside the securities industry, as reported by the broker

Any customer disputes or regulatory and disciplinary events on the broker's record.

The SEC's IAPD Program

The IAPD Program provides information about both SEC- and state-registered investment adviser firms. The SEC typically regulates investment advisers that manage more than $100 million in assets. Advisers that do not meet this threshold generally are regulated by the states.

Through the IAPD, investors may:

Search for an investment adviser firm

Check the adviser's registration status

View the adviser's current disclosures made through its Form ADV filing

Link to a state regulator's website

Link to the FINRA BrokerCheck website.

Investment adviser firms that have not registered with the SEC electronically will not appear on the IAPD page. If you do not see a firm listed through IAPD and you want to check the firm's registration status, contact the SEC at (202) 551-6825 or the appropriate state securities authority through http://www.nasaa.org.

Information on individual investment advisers is available through state securities regulators.

http://www.sec.gov/answers/crd.htm, January 28, 2015